THE DIABETES COOKBOOK
FOR THE WHOLE FAMILY

THE DIABETES COOKBOOK
FOR THE WHOLE FAMILY

2ND EDITION

MELISSA ARMSTRONG
JILL GOSPER AND EILEEN BURR
And all the Staff of the Diabetes Centre
St Vincent's Hospital, Sydney
A Principal Facility of the Sisters of Charity Health Service

SIMON & SCHUSTER
AUSTRALIA

The Diabetes Cookbook for the Whole Family 2nd edition is endorsed by Diabetes Australia, which is the national coordinating body of the diabetes movement, and is made up of thirteen member organisations with a combined membership of over 40,000 people. It provides a unique partnership between consumers—the people with diabetes—research organisations, doctors and other health professionals with a special interest in diabetes.

THE DIABETES COOKBOOK FOR THE WHOLE FAMILY
First published in Australasia in 1991 by
Simon & Schuster Australia
20 Barcoo Street, East Roseville NSW 2069

Reprinted 1991, 1992 (twice), 1993, 1994 (twice), 1995, 1996, 1997, 1998
This new edition first published in 1999

A Viacom Company
Sydney New York London Toronto Tokyo Singapore

National Library of Australia
Cataloguing in Publication data

Gosper, Jill.
Diabetes cookbook

2nd rev. ed.
Bibliography.
Includes index.
ISBN 0 7318 0844 4.

1. Diabetes - Diet therapy - Recipes. I. Burr, Eileen. II. Armstrong, Melissa. III. Title.

641.56314

Cover photograph: Louise Lister
Art direction (cover): Yolande Gray
Food styling (cover): Michelle Norianto
Illustrations: Katie Jordan
Design (cover and pages): Green Words and Images
Set in 11/13.5 Garamond

Printed in Australia by Southwood Press Pty Ltd

10 9 8 7 6 5 4 3

ACKNOWLEDGMENTS

The Diabetes Centre wishes to thank all those involved in the first edition of *The Diabetes Cookbook for the Whole Family*: Eileen Burr, Jill Gosper, Claire Hampton, Judy Reinhardt, Lesley Campbell, Don Chisholm, Brenda Adams, Raya Fertman, Sima Katman, Caroline Burr, Ernst & Young, Ian Johnston, Annette Bennett, Susan Morris-Yates, Christine Josephson, Bunty Kennard, Jonathan Chester, Lucy Andrews.

In addition we would like to thank the following for their assistance in the development of the second edition: Melissa Armstrong, Valerie Roberts, Ann-Marie Tannebek, Meegan Watts.

Further support was also provided by Australian Pork Corporation; Dairy Foods Advisory Bureau; Diabetes Australia (NSW); H. J. Heinz & Company Australia Limited; Kellogg (Australia) Pty Ltd; NSW Fish Marketing Authority; Searle Australia Pty Ltd; Accoutrement, Mosman; The Bay Tree, Woollahra; Butler & Co, Chatswood; Mosmania, Mosman; Powder Blue, Mosman; Villa Italiana, Mosman.

The original impetus for writing this cookbook came when Eileen Burr's son Alex was diagnosed with diabetes. During this stressful time, Eileen realised that there was a lack of a family-friendly cookbook to help prepare interesting meals, as well as to have these meals fit in with a healthy eating plan. Together with the staff and other friends of St Vincent's Hospital Diabetes Centre the first Diabetes Centre cookbook was created! Now nearly 10 years and 10 reprints later it was felt that a revamp was needed! Some of your favourite recipes remain but over 30 new recipes are now included to tempt all your family. We hope you enjoy the new edition of *The Diabetes Cookbook for the Whole Family*.

FOREWORD

Diet is the cornerstone in the management of diabetes mellitus. With this in mind, Eileen Burr, the mother of a boy recently diagnosed with diabetes, and the team at the Diabetes Centre at St Vincent's Hospital in Sydney wrote the first edition of this cookbook in 1989 to help people with diabetes continue to find enjoyment in their meals, while doing the best for the whole family's health. Since then, nutritional research, some of which I have been directly involved in, has already influenced the dietary rules that were current at the time. This has led to the acceptance of a much wider range of food choices to help in the achievement of healthy outcomes in diabetes mellitus.

The community has also developed a more cosmopolitan approach to food, necessitating changes in the types of recipes and advice about recipe modification. Melissa Armstrong, together with the rest of the St Vincent's Hospital Diabetes Centre Team, has created a book of tempting, up-to-date recipes. The Team has done a wonderful job incorporating the latest scientific understanding about nutrition in diabetes with advice that will help people with diabetes, whether newly diagnosed or longstanding, to enjoy healthy and nutritious meals.

Associate Professor Lesley Campbell
Director
St Vincent's Hospital Diabetes Centre
Sydney, 1999

CONTENTS

Recipes

INTRODUCTION

Good nutrition is an important part of diabetes management, but the healthiest food in the world isn't much help if it doesn't taste good! As dietitians we try very hard to teach people about healthy eating and also to help them to continue their enjoyment of food and eating. This updated version of our cookbook is part of that commitment. We would like to start our book by describing some of the basic principles of healthy eating and by bringing everyone with diabetes up to date on the latest thinking in regard to the best diet to follow.

It is, however, always important to bear in mind that nutrition is a scientific discipline and, for that reason, new research findings may result in a change of advice during a lifetime with diabetes. Perhaps some people reading this book will be surprised at how advice has changed already—there is sugar in some of our recipes—even though they may have been diagnosed with diabetes for only a few years. It is a good idea to have contact with a nutrition expert, i.e. dietitian, every couple of years to keep up to date with the latest discoveries. Also, there are many new food products appearing on our supermarket shelves and regular advice can help with keeping up with changes in this area.

ENERGY

The word energy has many meanings, but, in the nutritional sense, energy is a measure of the fuel that the body needs to function properly. To use an analogy, food is like petrol in a car. The car cannot run without petrol; the body cannot function without food. Likewise, if the wrong sort of petrol is put into the car, the performance will be affected. If a person eats the wrong food, the same thing will result—poor performance. The amount of energy the body requires is based on body size, exercise level and age group. Too little energy intake results in weight loss, while excess energy intake causes weight gain. Energy is measured in kilojoules (kJ) in the metric system or in kilocalories (kCal) in the imperial system. Remember: everyone is different and there is not a universal energy level.

PROTEIN

Protein is the name given to a particular food component whose role in the body is for growth and tissue repair. For example, protein forms new skin to heal a cut. Fingernails, hair and muscle are made of protein. Very little protein is required in the diet every day because the body recycles much of its protein. Contrary to what our mothers or grandmothers told us, large amounts of protein are not needed to build big, strong muscles. What is needed is exercise to build the muscles from the protein that is already available. Good food sources of protein are meat, chicken, fish, eggs, cheese, yoghurt, milk, legumes and nuts. These foods also provide essential vitamins and minerals, e.g. thiamine (vitamin B1) and iron. Unfortunately, except for legumes, they are also good sources of fat.

FAT

Fat is the part of food which provides the most concentrated energy. If more energy is eaten than is needed, the body stores it as fat for later use. Some body fat is essential to surround and protect important organs, such as the kidneys, and also as a source of some hormones. Animals, like humans, store fat and this is why food from animals contains fat. Fat is also present in seeds and nuts to give energy to the new plant when it starts to grow. Fat from food carries vitamins, e.g. vitamins A, D, E and K, which make fat an essential part of our diet.

Fat in food is described by its chemical structure as polyunsaturated, monounsaturated and saturated. These different types of fat are found in different proportions in different foods. As a general rule, foods that are animal in origin, e.g. meat and dairy products, contain mostly saturated fat. Fats from fruit or vegetable sources, e.g. olives, sunflowers and avocados, contain mono-unsaturated or polyunsaturated fats.

CARBOHYDRATE

Foods which contain carbohydrate provide the most readily available and preferred source of energy: glucose. Every cell in the body uses glucose. Some tissues, e.g. the brain, use glucose exclusively. As body cells, and we have billions of them, require glucose as a form of energy, it is essential that there is sufficient carbohydrate food in your diet every day to keep the body running efficiently. In fact, it is preferable to have these foods at every meal, i.e. spaced out across the day to provide the body with a steady source of fuel.

Carbohydrate foods are sometimes divided into starches and sugars, but their effects on the body are surprisingly similar to one another. Many carbohydrate-containing foods also contain fibre and are good sources of vitamins.

FIBRE

Fibre is the indigestible part of the food which passes right through the digestive system. Fibre helps regular bowel function and may help protect against bowel cancer. As fibre is not digested, it leaves a feeling of fullness after eating. This can be very useful for those trying to lose weight or who struggle with hunger pangs only 1–2 hours after eating.

When increasing the fibre content of your diet, it is best to do so slowly as increased fibre intake does mean increased gas production in the bowel, resulting in flatulence. If fibre is increased slowly, this problem is less troublesome as the bowel has time to adapt to its new diet. Fibre-rich foods include legumes, vegetables, fruit, breads and cereals.

VITAMINS

Vitamins regulate essential body functions and without them deficiency diseases can develop. However, some vitamins can be toxic if taken in large quantities, e.g. Vitamin A.

Sufficient vitamins can be obtained from eating a wide variety of fruit, vegetables and animal products. Vitamin supplements should only be taken if your diet is inadequate. The majority of Australians do not have vitamin deficiency problems. Recently, it has been recommended that all women contemplating pregnancy should take a daily folic acid supplement to reduce the risk of having a child with a neural tube defect, such as spina bifida. If in doubt about your need for a vitamin supplement, discuss this with your dietitian or doctor.

MINERALS

Minerals, like vitamins, are usually needed by the body in small quantities. The exception to this is calcium, which is the main component of bones and teeth. Different foods contain different minerals and so a diet with plenty of variety will provide all the minerals required.

If any of the food groups are avoided, mineral deficiencies may occur, e.g. if dairy foods are avoided completely, the body will not have sufficient calcium to build and maintain strong, healthy bones. Alternative sources of calcium would need to be included in the diet instead, e.g. calcium-enriched soy products.

DIETARY GUIDELINES FOR DIABETES

The dietary guidelines for people with diabetes are the same as those for all Australian people. The best diet for people with diabetes is also ideal for lowering cholesterol and reducing the risk of some cancers, such as bowel cancer and breast cancer.

The first Australian dietary guidelines were released in April 1979 and were revised in the early 1990s. The revised guidelines were launched by the National Health and Medical Research Council (NHMRC) in 1992. These guidelines summarise healthy eating for all Australians, especially people with diabetes.

Dietary Guidelines for Australians (1992)

1. Enjoy a wide variety of nutritious food.
2. Eat plenty of breads and cereals (preferably wholegrain), vegetables (including legumes) and fruit.
3. Eat a diet low in fat, particularly saturated fat.
4. Maintain a healthy body weight by balancing physical activity and food intake.
5. Limit alcohol intake.
6. Eat only a moderate amount of food containing added sugars.
7. Choose low-salt foods and use salt sparingly.
8. Encourage and support breastfeeding.

Guidelines on Specific Nutrients

1. Eat food containing calcium. This is particularly important for girls and women.
2. Eat food containing iron. This is especially important for girls, women, vegetarians and athletes.

Dietary Guidelines for Children

1. Encourage and support breastfeeding.
2. Enjoy a wide variety of nutritious food.
3. Eat plenty of breads and cereals (preferably wholegrain), vegetables (including legumes) and fruit.
4. Low-fat diets are not suitable for children. For older children, a diet low in fat and in particular, low in saturated fat, is appropriate.
5. Maintain a healthy body weight by balancing physical activity and food intake.
6. Water is the preferred drink for children; alcohol is not recommended.
7. Eat only a moderate amount of sugars and food containing added sugars.
8. Choose low-salt food and use salt sparingly.

Guidelines on Specific Nutrients

1. Eat food containing calcium.
2. Eat food containing iron.

Let's look at each of these points in turn, with some practical advice to help achieve these goals.

1. Enjoy a wide variety of nutritious food

By eating from all the food groups and having a variety of foods from those groups, adequate intake of vitamins and minerals will be ensured.

2. Eat plenty of breads and cereals (preferably wholegrain), vegetables (including legumes) and fruit

Remember carbohydrates—the body's essential fuel source. The following foods are packed full of carbohydrates: breads, cereals, vegetables and fruit. These should form the basic structure of your diet. They are very low in fat (unless it has been added) and are full of fibre, vitamins and minerals.

3. Eat a diet low in fat, particularly saturated fat

When fat is eaten, it makes body fat and cholesterol. When too much fat is eaten, too much body fat and cholesterol can be produced. Add only small amounts of fat-containing foods to the basic structure of breads, cereals, vegetables and fruit. Saturated fats (usually from animal sources) make cholesterol more easily than other fats, so reducing intake of this type of fat is especially important.

4. Maintain a healthy body weight by balancing physical activity and food intake

Body weight is a balance between how much food is eaten and how much exercise is done. Eat more and/or exercise less and body weight increases. Eat less and/or exercise more and your body weight decreases. Obviously, if you are trying to lose weight, a combination of increased exercise and decreased food intake will result in a larger and quicker weight loss.

5. Limit alcohol intake

Alcohol contains a large amount of energy (kJ/kCal) and can contribute to an excess of body fat. Large quantities of alcohol, either consumed daily or in binges, can damage almost every organ in the body. Safe levels of alcohol intake have been suggested by the National Health and Medical Research Council (NHMRC), i.e. less than/equal to 4 standard drinks per day for men and less than/equal to 2 drinks per day for women, with one alcohol-free day per week.

A standard drink is:
1 x 120 ml = 4 fl oz (one glass) of wine = 1 middy beer = 1 schooner of low-alcohol beer = 1 nip (30 ml = 1 fl oz) spirits = 60 ml (2 fl oz) fortified wine, e.g. sherry.

6. Eat only a moderate amount of food containing added sugars

Excessive quantities of sugar will cause large rises in blood glucose levels. Small quantities of sugar have little effect.

7. Choose low-salt foods and use salt sparingly

In susceptible individuals, a large salt intake is linked to high blood pressure. Unfortunately, it is impossible know who is sensitive and who is not. So a general guideline has been developed for everyone. Try first adding a little salt into cooking, but leaving that salt shaker in the kitchen so no more is added at the table. Choose salt-free/reduced-salt packaged foods where possible.

8. Encourage and support breastfeeding

Breastfeeding offers advantages to both mothers and babies.

Breastmilk is produced specifically to facilitate the healthy growth and development of babies. It is a complete food for the first 4–6 months of life. Breastmilk protects babies against infections and breastfeeding can help a mother's body return to normal again after the birth (although this can take up to 12 months). Breastmilk is also immediately available, takes no preparation time and is cheaper than bottle feeding.

It is understood that some mothers are unable to breastfeed for various reasons. These mothers are advised to use specialised commercial infant formulas to replace the breastmilk.

SPECIFIC NUTRIENTS

1. Eat food containing calcium

A good calcium intake throughout life will help to develop strong healthy bones and ensure peak adult bone mass is achieved. Good sources include dairy products, calcium-enriched soy products, leafy green vegetables, nuts.

2. Eat food containing iron

Iron helps carry oxygen around the body— what could be more important than that? Red meat is an excellent source of iron and it is also found in legumes, wholegrain cereals and some vegetables in smaller amounts. Foods containing vitamin C, e.g. fruit, help the body absorb iron, especially from those non-meat sources. People who eat little or no red meat need to ensure that they receive adequate iron intake by eating a variety of wholegrain cereals and legumes.

LET'S GO SHOPPING

The most important knowledge you need when you hit the supermarket is how to read food labels. If you are able to decipher the information given on the label, you will be able to choose the correct food very easily.

WHAT GOES ON A FOOD LABEL?

- The label must be legible, easily visible and in English.
- Nothing false or misleading can be contained on the label.
- The name of the food must be given.
- A list of ingredients in descending order of weight (except water) must be provided.
- Any additives to the food must be listed.
- The country in which the food was made must be given or a statement made that the ingredients are imported.
- The name of the manufacturer/importer/packer/vendor must be included.
- Date marking must be used to indicate the food's minimum durable life.
- If a nutrition claim is made, e.g. low-fat, then a nutrition panel must be shown to complement this claim.

HOW TO COMPARE BRANDS

By checking the nutritional information under 'per 100 g' on the packaging, it is possible to compare different products even though they come in a varied range of serving sizes. Pick the product with the least fat or look for products with less than 10 g fat per 100 g.

Carbohydrate

Total: This includes sugars and starches. If you are on an 'exchange' or 'portion' diet, you can work out how many 'exchanges' you are eating.

Sugars: This will include added sugars as well as the naturally occurring sugars in milk (lactose) and fruit (fructose). Cross-check with the ingredients list to find the source(s) of sugar. For instance, if a cereal contains sultanas, a higher sugar content is acceptable.

Dietary fibre

Once again use the figure 'per 100 g' and pick the one with the highest amount of fibre.

Sodium (salt)

Where possible, choose products with reduced or no added salt.

NUTRITION CLAIMS— WHAT THEY REALLY MEAN

Light or 'lite'

The characteristic which makes the food 'light' must be stated on the label, e.g. 'light' olive oil is either paler in colour or less strong-tasting than other olive oils, it is not lower in energy (kJ/kCal) than other olive oils. In other foods like potato chips, 'lite' can mean a low-salt product. If the term refers to the energy (kJ/kCal) content of the food, it must comply with the Food Standards Code.

Diet

This term has been used by food companies to imply that the product has a particular nutritional property. It is most often used to describe products whose energy (kJ/kCal) content is lower than other similar foods. This usage is now covered by the Food Standards Code to ensure the word 'diet' is always used in this context.

No added sugar

This means no added or additional sugar, e.g. glucose, honey, fructose, etc. However, this does not always mean it will contain less energy (kJ/kCal) as many foods are naturally high in sugar. Again, cross-check by referring to the nutrition panel.

Cholesterol-free

Cholesterol is only found in products of animal origin. For instance, avocados have always and will always be cholesterol-free. Importantly, cholesterol-free does not mean fat-free.

Low-fat

This term can only be used when the food contains less than 3 g fat per 100 g.

Low-joule

This term usually means that the food has been artificially sweetened.

No added salt

This term means salt has not been added to the food, but does not mean that the food has no salt in it.

High-fibre

The food must contain at least 3 g fibre per average serve.

The National Heart Foundation (NHF) has developed the 'Pick the Tick' campaign to help people choose low-fat, low-salt food. This can be very helpful when choosing food at the supermarket. However, many suitable foods do not pay to display the NHF tick. With good food-label reading skills, it is possible to choose the right foods, tick or no tick.

MORE INFORMATION ABOUT SUGAR IN YOUR DIET

It is in this area that advice has changed most over the years. Small quantities of sugar do not cause a rapid and uncontrollable rise in blood glucose levels. Very strict avoidance of sugar in a diabetic meal plan is not necessary. Perhaps you have noticed this yourself and it is no real news to you. For others, this may seem like heresy. This new advice about sugar comes from research which has determined the blood glucose raising effects of many different foods in actual people, including adults with diabetes. We now understand that different carbohydrate-containing foods are digested at different rates and so have different effects on blood glucose levels. This measure of the effect on blood glucose levels is called the glycaemic index (GI) of a food. These experiments have shown that small quantities of sugar do not cause big rises in blood glucose levels.

The key point here is the quantity of sugar, rather than whether to have sugar or not. For example, it is very sensible to avoid soft drinks and cordials which contain a lot of sugar in a relatively small volume, e.g. there are approximately 11 teaspoons of sugar in each can of lemonade or cola drink. If only one lolly or a small piece of chocolate is eaten, the effect on the blood glucose level is small; if half a packet is eaten, the effect will be large!

Many people with diabetes have deprived themselves of excellent packaged or processed foods in the mistaken belief that 'any sugar is too much sugar'. Dietitians now agree that the majority of breakfast cereals and many biscuits are suitable in a diabetic meal plan. Look for cereals that are low in fat and high in fibre, rather than being too worried about the sugar content.

It is important to remember that although the sugar may not make the blood glucose levels rise, it still contains energy (kJ/kCal) and this should be taken into consideration when trying to lose weight.

For more information on the glycaemic index we recommend the book: *The GI Factor* (2nd ed.) by Jennie Brand-Miller, Steve Colaguri and Kay Foster-Powell. It is available in most bookshops.

WHAT'S IN THE PANTRY?

Keeping a supply of basics in your pantry makes it much easier to create quick and easy meals. Here are some ideas and items to keep available.

- Wholegrain/wholemeal bread, rolls, muffins, crumpets, pocket pita, Lebanese or Turkish bread.
- High-fibre breakfast cereals, rolled oats, low-fat/low-sugar breakfast and muesli bars. Crackers, plain, sweet biscuits, popping corn, baked pretzels.
- Pasta—all shapes and sizes, rice—all types: long grain, arborio, quick cook, brown, jasmine, basmati, etc.
- Canned vegetables e.g. corn, tomatoes, asparagus, beetroot, beans.
- Dried fruit, fruit bars and fruit straps.
- Canned salmon, tuna, mackerel, sardines in brine or tomato sauce.
- No-oil dressings and low-fat mayonnaise.

- Canned/packet soups, tomato-based pasta sauces, packet sauces/casserole/stir-fry mixes.
- Curry pastes, e.g. Indian or Thai.
- Canned evaporated skim milk, 'lite' coconut cream, skim milk powder, long-life low-fat milks, low-joule cordials, soft drinks, jellies and toppings.
- Meat and fish paste, Vegemite™ and peanut butter, 100% fruit jams.
- Sick day or 'hypo' kit: jelly beans, glucose tablets, ordinary soft drink, honey, long-life fruit juice, ordinary jelly.

For the Fridge/Freezer

- Low-fat flavoured and natural yoghurt.
- Low-fat cheddar cheese, cheese slices, cottage or ricotta cheese.
- Low-fat ice cream.
- Low-fat crumbed fish fillets.
- Low-fat oven chips.
- Freshly cooked rice or wheat-flour noodles.

ADAPTING YOUR OWN RECIPES

There are many simple changes that can be made to your favourite recipes to make them more suitable for a healthy eating plan. Below are a number of ideas to try.

Reducing fat

- The most suitable cooking methods are those that require minimal or no fat to be added, i.e. grilling, poaching, boiling, steaming, barbecuing, microwaving, stir frying or dry roasting.
- If frying, use a non-stick pan or a little vegetable oil spray to stop the food from sticking. Spray oil can be used on grill plates, cake/muffin tins, barbecues, woks, etc.

- If baking, the non-stick baking paper Gladbake™ is an alternative to greasing the tray.
- When baking meat or chicken, put it on a rack in the baking dish. Pour approximately half a cup of water into the tray. This will provide moisture during cooking and help prevent the meat from drying out.
- Reduce the amount of fat or oil suggested for frying, e.g. an onion needs a teaspoon of oil to cook, not a tablespoon. Alternatively, don't fry the onion at all, but soften in water and tomato juice.
- Extend casseroles by substituting a quarter of the meat with legumes, i.e. kidney beans, lentils, chick peas.
- Reduce the quantity of meat or chicken in a recipe. Use only 125 g raw weight per person in casseroles, stir fries, etc.
- Skim the fat from casseroles and soups after cooking.
- Always use reduced-fat cheese to replace cheddar cheese in recipes, e.g. cheese sauce. For a little extra flavour add a tablespoon of parmesan cheese, only 3 g fat, but lots of taste!
- Replace full-cream milk and yoghurt with a low-fat variety.
- Use a low-fat evaporated milk instead of cream.
- Use low-fat yoghurt instead of sour cream. Reheat gently after adding the yoghurt to prevent curdling.

Adding flavour

- Be adventurous with the use of herbs and spices to add extra flavour to low-fat meals.
- Marinating meat and poultry helps to keep them tender and adds extra flavour.

- When stir frying try using small quantities of aromatic oils, e.g. sesame, chilli, etc. Use stock, salt-reduced soy sauce and/or sherry to give extra liquid.

Adding fibre

- Substitute half the white flour with wholemeal flour. The recipe may require a little extra liquid to be added to keep the product moist.
- Use brown rice and wholemeal pasta as accompaniments.
- Use fruit as a basis for desserts and sweet-tasting snacks. Add grated apple, grated carrot, mashed pumpkin, dates or banana to recipes for naturally sweet and moist cakes.

Now, on to our recipes for lots of interesting meals and snacks!

RECIPE CRITERIA

Fat

Negligible = less than/equal to 1 g/serve
Low   = 1–3 g/serve
Moderate = 3–6 g/serve

Fibre

Negligible = less than/equal to 1 g/serve
Low   = 1–3 g/serve
Good   = 3–6 g/serve
Very good = greater than 6 g/serve

BREAKFAST IDEAS

Nowadays not everyone has time for a traditional breakfast. Some of our ideas are for breakfast on the run and some are more suitable to weekends and holidays when there may be more time to spend on preparation. Some of these recipes could also be used for a quick lunch or evening meal.

ORANGE AND APRICOT PUNCH

Recipe courtesy of Dairy Foods Advisory Bureau

6 tinned apricot halves (no added sugar)
200 mg (6$^1/_2$ oz) low-fat apricot yoghurt
$^1/_2$ cup buttermilk
$^1/_2$ cup orange juice

1. Purée apricots with yoghurt.

2. Add buttermilk and orange juice, and blend together.

Makes 2 large servings	
Kilojoules per serve	790
Calories per serve	189
Carbohydrate per serve	30 g
Fat	Low
Fibre	Good

PEACHY PICK-ME-UP

Recipe courtesy of Dairy Foods Advisory Bureau

425 g (13$^1/_2$ oz) canned peach slices (no added sugar)

200 g (6$^1/_2$ oz) natural low-fat yoghurt

$^1/_2$ cup skim milk, chilled until icy

$^1/_2$ tsp ground ginger

1 tbsp wheat germ (optional)

Makes 2 large servings	
Kilojoules per serve	563
Calories per serve	135
Carbohydrate per serve	20 g
Fat	Low
Fibre	Good

1. Purée or mash peaches.

2. Add remaining ingredients and blend until smooth.

ANN-MARIE'S MUESLI

4 cups rolled oats

$^1/_2$ cup wheat bran

$^1/_4$ cup oat or barley bran

$^1/_2$ cup lecithin

1 cup sultanas

1 cup slivered almonds

$^1/_4$ cup wheat germ

Makes 25 servings, 1 serve = $^1/_4$ cup	
Kilojoules per serve	605
Calories per serve	144
Carbohydrate per serve	17 g
Fat	Moderate
Fibre	Good

1. In a large bowl, combine all ingredients and mix well.

2. Transfer to an airtight container.

3. Serve with low-fat milk or yoghurt and fruit.

MICROWAVE CREAMY FRUIT PORRIDGE

1 cup quick-cook oats
1 cup hot water
1¹/₂ cups evaporated skim milk
4 cups sultanas or mixed dried fruit
2 ripe bananas
pinch ground cinnamon (optional)

Makes 4 servings	
Kilojoules per serve	1083
Calories per serve	258
Carbohydrate per serve	44 g
Fat	Low
Fibre	Good

1. In a large microwave bowl, combine oats, water and half the milk. Microwave on HIGH for 5 minutes.

2. Stir in dried fruit and remaining milk. Mash one banana and mix in well. Cook on HIGH for 1 minute.

3. Slice remaining banana and arrange on porridge. Sprinkle with cinnamon, if desired, and serve.

HAM AND CORN TOPPER

1 tsp canola oil
1 onion, finely chopped
4 slices lean ham, finely chopped
440 g (14 oz) canned creamed corn
440 g (14 oz) canned corn kernels, drained
2 tbsp chopped parsley
ground black pepper to taste

Makes 4 servings	
Kilojoules per serve	993
Calories per serve	236
Carbohydrate per serve	40 g
Fat	Low
Fibre	Very good

1. Heat oil in a small frying pan. Sauté onion and ham for 3 minutes, or until onion is transparent.

2. Add creamed corn and corn kernels and reheat.

3. Stir in parsley and pepper.

4. Serve on toast.

APPLE AND COTTAGE CHEESE TOAST

1 large or 2 small delicious apples, peeled, cored
and sliced

4 tbsp unsweetened orange juice

1 tsp lemon juice

$^1/_2$ cup water

200 g (6$^1/_2$ oz) low-fat cottage cheese

25 g (1 oz) crushed hazelnuts

2 tsp sugar

4 slices Vogel's Fruit 'n' Nut bread

$^1/_2$ tsp ground cinnamon

Makes 4 servings	
Kilojoules per serve	998
Calories per serve	236
Carbohydrate per serve	27 g
Fat	Moderate
Fibre	Good

1. In a saucepan, poach apple slices in orange juice, lemon juice and water for 10 minutes, or until apple is just soft.

2. Mix together cottage cheese, hazelnuts and half the sugar.

3. Toast bread until golden.

4. Spread cottage cheese mixture over toast.

5. Drain apple and arrange slices on top of toast. Sprinkle with cinnamon and remaining sugar.

6. Place under a hot grill until browned.

PEACH 'N' MANGO WHISK

1$^1/_4$ cups Kellogg's All-Bran™

140 g (4$^1/_2$ oz) canned peach and mango slices in
natural juice

2 tbsp low-fat vanilla yoghurt

$^3/_4$ cup low-fat milk, chilled until icy

pinch ground nutmeg

Makes 2 servings	
Kilojoules per serve	432
Calories per serve	103
Carbohydrate per serve	18 g
Fat	Negligible
Fibre	Moderate

1. Combine All-Bran™, peach and mango slices, yoghurt and milk in a blender.

2. Process for 30 seconds to 1 minute until drink becomes frothy.

3. Sprinkle with nutmeg and serve immediately.

SPICY SCRAMBLED EGGS WITH BEANS

canola oil spray
1 onion, finely chopped
1 clove garlic, crushed
6 eggs
3 tbsp skim milk
1 tbsp tomato sauce
$^1/_2$ tsp prepared mustard
425 g (13$^1/_2$ oz) canned baked beans
chopped parsley to garnish

Makes 4 servings	
Kilojoules per serve	664
Calories per serve	158
Carbohydrate per serve	10 g
Fat	Moderate
Fibre	Good

1. Spray a large saucepan with canola oil. Add onion and garlic and fry for 5 minutes, or until soft and transparent.

2. In a large bowl, beat together eggs, milk, tomato sauce and mustard.

3. Add to pan and cook over medium heat, stirring gently until mixture is set but soft.

4. In a separate saucepan, heat baked beans and arrange in a circle on a warmed serving dish. Pile scrambled eggs into the centre. Sprinkle with parsley and serve immediately.

SOUPS

With today's busy lifestyle, we often rely on pre-prepared convenience foods that can be cooked and served quickly without too much thought or fuss in the kitchen. Somehow, such meals don't always satisfy our desire for a good old-fashioned, home-cooked meal 'just like mother or grandmother used to make'. Memories of thick hearty soups with hot buttery toast can still tantalise the most sophisticated taste buds.

Our soup recipes have been chosen for their relatively easy preparation, nourishing ingredients and tasty satisfying combinations. Most are a meal in themselves.

EASY LENTIL SOUP

8 cups water
2 cups green lentils
1 medium onion, chopped
3 stalks celery, sliced
1 medium carrot, sliced
1 medium potato, sliced
3 leaves spinach, shredded
1 clove garlic, crushed
$\frac{1}{2}$ tsp oregano leaves
salt and pepper to taste

Makes 10 to 15 servings	
Kilojoules per serve	206
Calories per serve	49
Carbohydrate per serve	8 g
Fat	Negligible
Fibre	Good

1. Place all ingredients into a large saucepan.

2. Bring to the boil then reduce heat and simmer 30–45 minutes.

3. Adjust seasonings to taste.

GWEN'S CARROT AND ORANGE SOUP

3 cups fresh chicken stock (see recipe below)
1 cup orange juice
4 large carrots, chopped
1 medium onion, chopped
1 large leek, sliced
1 small bunch (4–5) shallots (green onions),
chopped
$^1/_2$ tsp nutmeg
$^1/_2$ tsp allspice

Makes 4 to 6 servings	
Kilojoules per serve	199
Calories per serve	47
Carbohydrate per serve	9 g
Fat	Negligible
Fibre	Excellent

1. Combine all ingredients in a large saucepan and boil over a moderate heat until vegetables are soft.

2. Pour into a blender and process until smooth.

3. Reheat to serve and add further seasoning if desired.

FRESH CHICKEN STOCK

1 boiling chicken (No. 13, 1.3 kg/2lb 1oz)
3 l (5 pt) water
3 large onions
bay leaves
$^1/_2$ bunch parsley
$^1/_2$ tbsp black peppercorns
$^1/_2$ tbsp salt

Makes 3 litres

1. Place chicken in a large saucepan with water, onions, herbs and seasonings.

2. Bring to the boil then reduce heat.

3. Cover and simmer for 2 hours, skimming surface throughout cooking time.

4. Allow to cook then remove chicken meat and bones.

5. Refrigerate overnight. Remove congealed fat and strain before using.

ALICE'S LENTIL AND BARLEY SOUP

4 rashers lean bacon, chopped (see Note)

1 large onion, chopped

2 cloves garlic, crushed

3 medium carrots, chopped

4 large tomatoes, chopped

1 cup green lentils, washed

1 cup barley, washed

1½ tsp mixed herbs

salt and ground black pepper to taste

4–6 cups water

Makes 6 to 8 servings	
Kilojoules per serve	732
Calories per serve	175
Carbohydrate per serve	28 g
Fat	Low
Fibre	Excellent

1. Preheat oven to 200°C (400°F).

2. Cook bacon in a non-stick frypan until crispy.

3. Remove bacon from pan and sauté onion and garlic, stirring frequently.

4. Add remaining vegetables and cook for 2 minutes. Return bacon to mixture.

5. In a large casserole combine lentils and barley, then add bacon mixture, herbs and seasonings to taste.

6. Cover with water and stir well.

7. Cook in the oven for 1½ hours. Add more water if necessary to obtain a thinner consistency.

Note: Bacon can be omitted if desired, therefore begin recipe at step 3, leaving out the bacon to make a vegetarian soup with a negligible fat content.

PUMPKIN SOUP

1 tbsp olive oil
1 medium butternut pumpkin, peeled and chopped
1 medium onion, chopped
2 stalks celery, chopped
2 cloves garlic, crushed
6 cups chicken or vegetable stock
grated rind and juice of 1 large orange
salt and ground black pepper to taste
natural yoghurt and orange rind for garnishing

Makes 10 servings	
Kilojoules per serve	300
Calories per serve	72
Carbohydrate per serve	9 g
Fat	Negligible
Fibre	Good

1. Heat oil in a large saucepan and add pumpkin, onion, celery and garlic.

2. Cover and cook over a moderate heat for about 5 minutes.

3. Add stock, replace cover and continue to cook for 25–30 minutes or until vegetables are tender.

4. Pour mixture into blender or food processor and blend until smooth.

5. Return to saucepan, add rind, orange juice and seasoning.

6. Reheat to serve hot, or chill and serve garnished with yoghurt and extra orange rind.

EASY FISH SOUP

1 large potato, finely chopped
2 shallots (green onions), finely chopped
1 leek, finely chopped
250 g (8 oz) fish fillets, such as ling, redfish
100 g (3½ oz) mussels, cleaned
3 cups fish stock or bouillon
1 cup dry white wine
pinch saffron threads
200 g (6½ oz) green prawns, shelled
salt and ground back pepper to taste

Makes 4 servings	
Kilojoules per serve	920
Calories per serve	219
Carbohydrate per serve	11 g
Fat	Low
Fibre	Low

1. Place potato, shallots, leek, fish and mussels in a large saucepan. Add stock and bring slowly to the boil.

2. In a separate saucepan, warm white wine with saffron for 2 minutes.

3. Add white wine and saffron to soup.

4. Add prawns and salt and pepper.

5. When mussels are open, the soup is ready to serve.

Note: Discard any mussels that do not open once cooked.

CREAMY CRAB CHOWDER

170 g (5½ oz) canned crab meat
1 large potato, peeled and sliced
1 stalk celery, chopped
1 small onion, chopped
salt and ground black pepper to taste
4 cups skim milk
2 tbsp skim-milk powder blended to a paste with a
little water

Makes 4 to 6 servings	
Kilojoules per serve	469
Calories per serve	112
Carbohydrate per serve	13 g
Fat	Low
Fibre	Good

1. Place crab, potato, celery, onion and seasonings in a saucepan with skim milk and skim-milk paste.

2. Bring to the boil then simmer over a low heat for 20–30 minutes or until potato is tender.

PEA AND VEAL BALL SOUP

1 cup green split peas
4 cups water
1 beef stock cube
2 stalks celery with leaves, chopped
1 medium onion, chopped
$^{1}/_{2}$ tsp dried basil
$^{1}/_{2}$ tsp dried marjoram
ground black pepper to taste
$^{1}/_{2}$ packet (125 g/4 oz) frozen spinach

Veal Balls
250 g (8 oz) minced veal
1 egg, beaten
$^{1}/_{4}$ cup dried breadcrumbs
$^{1}/_{2}$ tsp dried basil

Makes 6 servings	
Kilojoules per serve	564
Calories per serve	135
Carbohydrate per serve	11 g
Fat	Low
Fibre	Excellent

1. Place the peas and water in a large saucepan with stock cube, celery, onion, basil, marjoram and pepper.

2. Bring to the boil, reduce heat then simmer covered until peas are cooked to a mushy consistency—about 1 hour.

3. To make veal balls, combine veal with egg, breadcrumbs and basil then shape into walnut-sized balls.

4. Add the veal balls and spinach to soup and simmer for 25 minutes.

RAYA'S RUSSIAN BORSCHT

2 fresh beetroots, peeled
2 tomatoes, peeled and chopped
1 medium onion, chopped
1 stalk celery, chopped
4 cups water or stock
1 cup savoy cabbage, roughly chopped
2 medium potatoes, peeled and diced
1 medium carrot, peeled and grated
2 tbsp tomato paste
2 tbsp tomato sauce
salt and ground black pepper to taste

Makes 4 to 6 servings	
Kilojoules per serve	250
Calories per serve	60
Carbohydrate per serve	12 g
Fat	Negligible
Fibre	Excellent

1. Simmer the beetroots, tomatoes, onion and celery in the water or stock until tender—about 30–40 minutes.

2. Remove the beetroots and grate them.

3. Place the cabbage, potatoes, carrot, grated beetroot, tomato paste and tomato sauce into the stock. Season to taste.

4. Simmer for a further 30–40 minutes or until potatoes are tender.

SPRING SOUP

2 large carrots, peeled and sliced
1 small parsnip, peeled and sliced
1 small onion, halved and sliced
1 tbsp olive oil
6 cups chicken or vegetable stock
2 large potatoes, peeled and diced
1 packet (250 g/8 oz) frozen spinach, chopped
1 tbsp chopped parsley

Makes 4 to 6 servings	
Kilojoules per serve	251
Calories per serve	60
Carbohydrate per serve	10 g
Fat	Negligible
Fibre	Excellent

1. Sauté carrots, parsnip and onion in oil in a large saucepan.

2. Add stock and potatoes, bring to the boil then simmer for 5 minutes.

3. Stir in frozen spinach and simmer for a further 5–10 minutes.

4. Serve sprinkled with parsley.

SALADS AND VEGETABLES

'Rabbit' food is never boring when it's presented in colourful, crunchy, deliciously moist and tasty ways. Served hot or cold our vegetable recipes will add a refreshing taste to your meals and may even outshine the roast or grill you choose to serve them with.

SIMPLE SALAD CUPS

1 large carrot, diced
1 large potato, diced
$^1/_2$ cup frozen peas
1 red apple, peeled (p.14), cored and chopped
$^1/_2$ cup pecan nuts, chopped
$^1/_4$ cup low-joule salad dressing
4 lettuce leaves

Makes 4 servings	
Kilojoules per serve	465
Calories per serve	111
Carbohydrate per serve	10 g
Fat	Low
Fibre	Excellent

1. Steam or microwave carrot, potato and peas until just tender.

2. While still warm, toss through apple, pecan nuts and dressing.

3. Spoon into lettuce leaves. Chill before serving.

CHINESE NOODLE SALAD

375 g (12 oz) Hokkien noodles
¹/₄ bunch shallots (green onions), sliced diagonally
¹/₄ packet bean sprouts
¹/₂ cucumber, finely sliced
¹/₂ red capsicum, finely chopped
1 medium carrot, finely sliced
2 tbsp sesame seeds, toasted
3 tbsp slivered almonds, toasted

Makes 4 servings	
Kilojoules per serve	974
Calories per serve	232
Carbohydrate per serve	27 g
Fat	Moderate
Fibre	Good

1. In a large bowl, pour boiling water over noodles to cover and stand for 5 minutes. Drain, then rinse in cold water.

2. Combine noodles, shallots, bean sprouts, cucumber, red capsicum, carrot, sesame seeds and almonds on a large serving platter.

Dressing
1 tsp finely chopped fresh ginger
¹/₄ cup soy sauce
3 tbsp sweet chilli sauce
2 tbsp teriyaki sauce
1 tsp sesame oil
¹/₄ bunch fresh coriander, chopped

1. Combine all dressing ingredients, leaving some coriander for garnish, in a small jar. Shake well.

2. Pour dressing over noodles and toss well.

3. Garnish with remaining coriander.

SEA AND SUN

475 g (15 oz) canned Greenseas™ tuna in brine
440 g (14 oz) canned corn kernels
3 medium tomatoes, diced
1 cucumber, peeled and diced
1 stalk celery, finely sliced
1 small onion, finely chopped
5 black olives, chopped
1 cup chopped mushrooms
1 green capsicum, seeded and chopped
2 medium carrots, peeled and finely diced
³/₄ cup low-joule dressing (see Note)

Makes 6 to 8 servings	
Kilojoules per serve	705
Calories per serve	168
Carbohydrate per serve	19 g
Fat	Low
Fibre	Excellent

1. Drain tuna and corn. Place in a large salad bowl.

2. Toss with remaining vegetables and low-joule dressing.

3. Chill well before serving.

Note: Use Italian, herb and garlic, or French low-joule (no oil dressing) for this recipe.

BEAN AND APPLE SALAD

3 crisp red-skinned apples
1 tbsp lemon juice
440 g (14 oz) canned bean mix
3 stalks celery, sliced
200 g (6¹/₂ oz) natural low-fat yoghurt
2 tbsp low-oil mayonnaise
salt and pepper to taste

Makes 4 to 6 servings	
Kilojoules per serve	426
Calories per serve	102
Carbohydrate per serve	18 g
Fat	Negligible
Fibre	Excellent

1. Halve and core apples. Do not peel. Cut one half into slender wedges, dice the remainder.

2. Sprinkle lemon juice over apples, to prevent browning.

3. Combine diced apples, drained beans and celery in salad bowl.

4. Mix yoghurt with mayonnaise and seasonings. Pour over salad. Toss well.

5. Decorate with apple wedges. Chill well before serving.

GREEN AND GOLD SALAD

310 g (10 oz) canned unsweetened
mandarin segments
1 bunch English spinach, torn
1 small Spanish onion, sliced
$^1/_2$ cup slivered almonds, toasted
$^1/_2$ tsp mustard
2 tsp olive oil
1 tsp lemon juice
salt and ground pepper to taste

Makes 4 servings	
Kilojoules per serve	459
Calories per serve	110
Carbohydrate per serve	6 g
Fat	Moderate
Fibre	Excellent

1. Drain mandarin segments and reserve liquid.

2. Place mandarin segments, spinach, onion and almonds in a salad bowl.

3. Mix together reserved mandarin liquid with mustard, oil, lemon juice and seasonings. Chill, then pour over salad just before serving.

BUTTERMILK COLESLAW

$^1/_2$ medium cabbage, finely shredded
2 medium carrots, peeled and grated
1 large red capsicum, halved, finely sliced
3 stalks celery, chopped
$^1/_2$ cup chopped parsley
$1^1/_2$ cups buttermilk
$^1/_2$ cup concentrated orange juice
1 tbsp seed mustard
salt and ground pepper to taste

Makes 4 to 6 servings	
Kilojoules per serve	365
Calories per serve	87
Carbohydrate per serve	10 g
Fat	Low
Fibre	Excellent

1. Toss vegetables and parsley together in a large salad bowl.

2. Blend together buttermilk, orange juice, mustard and seasonings.

3. Mix dressing through cabbage mixture and allow to chill for 1–2 hours before serving.

PINEAPPLE SEASHELL SALAD

250 g (8 oz) shell macaroni, cooked
425 g (13^1/$_2$ oz) canned unsweetened pineapple
pieces, drained
1 cup cooked chicken or ham, chopped
1 medium cucumber, peeled, seeded and cubed
1 small red capsicum, cut into fine strips
4 shallots (green onions), finely chopped
200 g (6^1/$_2$ oz) natural low-fat yoghurt
salt and ground pepper to taste
lettuce leaves

Makes 6 servings	
Kilojoules per serve	1022
Calories per serve	244
Carbohydrate per serve	31 g
Fat	Low
Fibre	Excellent

1. Mix together macaroni shells, pineapple, chicken or ham, cucumber, capsicum and shallots.

2. Fold through yoghurt and seasonings to taste.

3. Serve in salad bowl lined with lettuce leaves.

EILEEN'S FAVOURITE SUMMER POTATOES

1 kg (2 lb) new potatoes
1 bunch shallots (green onions), finely chopped
4 stalks celery, finely chopped
2 large dill pickles, sliced
125 g (4 oz) light sour cream
3 tbsp white vinegar
salt and freshly ground black pepper to taste
^{1}/$_2$ tsp paprika
3 tbsp chopped parsley

Makes 6 servings	
Kilojoules per serve	644
Calories per serve	154
Carbohydrate per serve	24 g
Fat	Low
Fibre	Excellent

1. Boil unpeeled potatoes in lightly salted water until tender. Drain and cool.

2. Cut cooked potatoes into halves and place into a large salad bowl with shallots, celery and dill pickles.

3. Mix sour cream with vinegar and seasonings, then pour over warm potatoes.

4. Garnish with paprika and parsley.

5. Serve warm.

SAVOURY RICE BAKE

1 cup long-grain rice
1 onion, finely chopped
1 carrot, diced
2 stalks celery, sliced
$^1/_2$ cup raisins
1 vegetable or chicken stock cube
2 cups hot water
$^1/_2$ cup flaked almonds

Makes 4 servings	
Kilojoules per serve	1392
Calories per serve	331
Carbohydrate per serve	51 g
Fat	Moderate
Fibre	Very good

1. Place rice in a casserole dish.

2. Sprinkle onion, carrot, celery and raisins over rice.

3. Crumble stock cube into hot water, stir to dissolve, and pour over rice.

4. Cover and cook in moderate oven 180°C (350°F) for 45 minutes, or until rice is tender.

5. Fold almonds through and serve with grilled or barbecued beef or chicken.

MICROWAVE POTATO AND CARROT BAKE

500 g (1 lb) old potatoes, thinly sliced
2 leeks, thinly sliced
3 tomatoes, sliced
3 carrots, thinly sliced
$^1/_2$ cup chicken or vegetable stock
1 tbsp chopped parsley to garnish

Makes 4 servings	
Kilojoules per serve	536
Calories per serve	128
Carbohydrate per serve	25 g
Fat	Negligible
Fibre	Very good

1. Line a deep ovenproof dish with a layer of potatoes. Then add a layer of leeks, tomatoes and carrots.

2. Repeat layering until all vegetables are used, finishing with a layer of potatoes.

3. Pour stock over. Cover and cook in the microwave on HIGH for 15 minutes, or until vegetables are tender.

4. Sprinkle with parsley and serve with grilled or barbecued beef or chicken.

MUSHROOMS 'N' NOODLE TOSS

1 cup mushrooms, sliced

2 tsp olive oil

1 tbsp lemon juice

250 g (8 oz) pasta spirals, cooked

1 capsicum, quartered and sliced

1 tbsp dill, chopped

1 tbsp parsley, chopped

$^1/_4$ cup pine nuts

$^1/_2$ cup low-joule French dressing

Makes 4 to 6 servings	
Kilojoules per serve	690
Calories per serve	165
Carbohydrate per serve	23 g
Fat	Moderate
Fibre	Excellent

1. Sauté mushrooms in oil for 1 minute.

2. Stir in lemon juice and cook a further minute. Allow to cool.

3. Combine pasta, capsicum, dill, parsley, pine nuts and mushrooms in a large salad bowl. Cover and chill.

4. Toss with French dressing before serving.

SPICY CABBAGE

$^1/_2$ small red cabbage, shredded

2 apples, sliced

1 onion, halved and sliced

2 whole cloves

6 black peppercorns

$^1/_2$ tsp salt

1 cup water

$^1/_2$ cup apple juice

$1^1/_2$ tbsp vinegar

Makes 6 servings	
Kilojoules per serve	152
Calories per serve	36
Carbohydrate per serve	7 g
Fat	Negligible
Fibre	Excellent

1. Place all ingredients into a casserole dish.

2. Cover and bake at 200°C (400°F) for 30–40 minutes or until cabbage is soft.

3. Serve as an accompaniment to grilled or roast pork.

MICROWAVE ZUCCHINI WITH TOMATOES

1 tsp olive oil
1 onion, finely chopped
3 large or 4 medium zucchini, sliced
425 g (13¹/₂ oz) canned tomatoes with
herbs and garlic
2 tsp chilli sauce (optional)
ground black pepper to taste

Makes 4 servings	
Kilojoules per serve	225
Calories per serve	54
Carbohydrate per serve	6.9 g
Fat	Negligible
Fibre	Good

1. In a microwave dish, mix olive oil and onion and cook on HIGH for 1 minute, or until soft.

2. Add zucchini, tomatoes, chilli sauce and pepper. Stir well. Cover.

3. Cook in the microwave on HIGH for 15 minutes, or until zucchini is tender.

4. Transfer to a serving dish and serve hot or cold with grilled meat and potatoes.

LEMONY VEGETABLES WITH DILL

4 small new potatoes, halved
$^1/_2$ cup cubed butternut pumpkin
1 medium carrot, sliced
1 medium parsnip, sliced
1 small onion, cut into wedges
2 tsp margarine
1 tbsp cornflour
1 tbsp brown sugar
1 tbsp water
$^1/_4$ tsp lemon rind
2 tbsp lemon juice
2 tsp chopped dill

Makes 4 servings	
Kilojoules per serve	431
Calories per serve	103
Carbohydrate per serve	17.5 g
Fat	Low
Fibre	Good

1. Place potatoes, pumpkin, carrot, parsnip and onion in a microwave container with a small amount of water and cook in the microwave on HIGH until tender, about 8 minutes. Drain vegetables.

2. Melt margarine in a small saucepan over low heat and stir in the cornflour and brown sugar. Stir in water, lemon rind, lemon juice and dill.

3. Continue stirring until mixture boils and thickens. Cook for a further 2 minutes.

4. Pour glaze over drained vegetables and reheat in the microwave for 1–2 minutes.

5. Serve with grilled or barbecued beef or chicken.

SWEET AND SOUR VEGETABLE SAUCE

2 tsp olive oil
1 onion, cut into wedges
1 green capsicum, sliced
1 large carrot, cut into sticks
1 cup broccoli florets
425 g (13 1/2 oz) canned unsweetened pineapple pieces
1 small tin water chestnuts, drained and sliced
1 tbsp soy sauce
3 tbsp tomato sauce
2 tbsp white vinegar
2 tbsp cornflour
1/2 cup water

Makes 4 servings	
Kilojoules per serve	671
Calories per serve	160
Carbohydrate per serve	30 g
Fat	Low
Fibre	Excellent

1. Heat oil, then sauté onion, capsicum, carrot and broccoli for 3–4 minutes.

2. Add pineapple with the juice, water chestnuts, soy sauce, tomato sauce, vinegar and combined cornflour and water.

3. Bring to the boil and stir until thickened.

4. Serve with brown rice or Chinese noodles.

MARINATED BUTTON MUSHROOMS

500 g (1 lb) button mushrooms
pinch thyme
1 bay leaf, crumbled
1 small clove garlic, crushed
1 small onion, sliced
4 tbsp vinegar
1 tsp olive oil
1/2 tsp salt and 1/2 tsp sugar

Makes 4 to 6 servings	
Kilojoules per serve	112
Calories per serve	27
Carbohydrate per serve	1 g
Fat	Negligible
Fibre	Good

1. Combine all ingredients in a saucepan.

2. Bring to the boil then simmer gently for 6–8 minutes.

3. Pour into suitable container, cover, then store in refrigerator for 2–3 hours or overnight, before serving as a snack or hors d'oeuvre.

LEGUMES

Many people avoid bean recipes either because they believe they take too long to prepare, or because they dislike the taste and texture. We hope we can change your mind with these simple and very tasty dishes.

Beans, peas and lentils are all legumes, and are all rich in complex carbohydrates and fibre, low in fat, and provide vitamins and minerals, including iron. When combined with a grain, e.g. wheat, such as in a meal of Heinz™ Baked Beans on toast, the protein content is as valuable as that provided in servings of meat, eggs or fish. Many recent studies have proved that when eaten in conjunction with a low-fat diet, beans can help to lower blood cholesterol levels.

Try them fresh, frozen, dried or canned to add interest and economical nutrition to your family meals.

MIA'S FAVA

250 g (8 oz) yellow split peas
1$^1/_2$ tsp olive oil
1 large onion
400 ml (13 fl oz) vegetable stock
2 tbsp soy sauce
50 g (1$^1/_2$ oz) feta cheese, crumbled

Makes 4 servings	
Kilojoules per serve	1027
Calories per serve	245
Carbohydrate per serve	30 g
Fat	Moderate
Fibre	Very good

1. In a large bowl, soak split peas overnight in enough water to cover.

2. Heat olive oil in a large saucepan, add onion and cook until soft, about 5 minutes.

3. Add split peas, stock and soy sauce. Cook until split peas are soft, about 30 minutes. Stir occasionally to prevent sticking.

4. When cooked, transfer to a blender and process for 2 minutes, or until smooth.

5. Sprinkle with feta cheese.

6. Serve with chopped tomatoes, cucumber, lettuce and crusty bread.

VEAL AND BEAN COBBLER

500 g (1 lb) minced veal
2 stalks celery, chopped
1 onion, chopped
1 capsicum, chopped
1 clove garlic, crushed
$^1/_2$ tsp salt
1 tsp paprika
440 g (14 oz) canned bean mix, drained and rinsed
350 g (11 oz) canned black-eyed beans, drained and rinsed
4 tbsp tomato paste
2 cups water

Makes 6 servings	
Kilojoules per serve	1350
Calories per serve	322
Carbohydrate per serve	31 g
Fat	Moderate
Fibre	Excellent

1. Brown veal with celery, onion, capsicum, garlic, salt and paprika in a non-stick pan over a high heat, stirring constantly.

2. Reduce heat and stir in beans, tomato paste and water.

3. Simmer for 30 minutes.

4. Place two-thirds of the meat mixture into a casserole dish. Cool remaining third.

Scone Dough
$1^1/_2$ cups plain flour
2 tsp baking powder
60 g (2 oz) margarine
$^1/_2$ cup skim milk

1. Sift dry ingredients, then rub through margarine with fingertips until mixture resembles fine breadcrumbs.

2. Stir in enough milk to make a soft dough then roll out to a rectangle 30 x 20 cm (12 x 8 in.).

3. Spread cooled meat mixture over scone dough then roll up from long side.

4. Cut into 1.5 cm ($^1/_2$ in.) slices then arrange these over the meat mixture in casserole dish.

5. Bake in a hot oven 200°C (400°F) for 10–15 minutes.

LENTIL CURRY

3 tbsp curry paste
1 onion, finely chopped
425 g (13$^1/_2$ oz) canned tomatoes, crushed
1 cup red lentils, rinsed
2$^1/_2$ cups boiling water

Makes 4 servings	
Kilojoules per serve	777
Calories per serve	185
Carbohydrate per serve	20 g
Fat	Moderate
Fibre	Very good

1. In a medium saucepan, heat curry paste until aromatic, about 2 minutes. Sauté onion in curry paste until soft, then add tomatoes.

2. Place lentils in saucepan with boiling water. Bring to the boil. Reduce heat and simmer gently for 20–25 minutes, or until lentils are soft. Stir regularly to stop lentils sticking to bottom of the saucepan.

3. Add cooked lentils to onion mixture and stir well.

4. Reheat until curry boils and thickens.

5. Serve with basmati rice, plain low-fat yoghurt and salad.

TOMATO CHILLI BEANS

1 clove garlic, crushed
1 small onion, finely chopped
1 stalk celery, chopped
1 tsp olive oil
425 g (13½ oz) canned tomatoes, roughly
chopped, with liquid
1 tbsp tomato paste
2 x 420 g (13¼ oz) canned 3-bean mix, drained and rinsed
1 tbsp sweet chilli sauce
½ tsp finely chopped fresh chilli (optional)
1 green capsicum, chopped
¼ cup grated low-fat cheddar cheese
pinch ground paprika

Makes 4 servings as a side dish	
Kilojoules per serve	1058
Calories per serve	252
Carbohydrate per serve	35 g
Fat	Low
Fibre	Very good

1. Combine garlic, onion, celery and olive oil in a large microwave dish.

2. Cook in the microwave on HIGH for 3 minutes.

3. Add chopped tomatoes and juice, tomato paste, 3-bean mix, chilli sauce, fresh chilli, if desired, and capsicum. Stir together well.

4. Return to microwave and cook on HIGH for a further 5 minutes, or until mixture boils.

5. Top with cheese, sprinkle with paprika, then cook on HIGH for 2 minutes, or until cheese is melted.

6. Serve with grilled or barbecued beef or chicken.

SUPER BEAN MEAT LOAF

500 g (1 lb) minced veal
1 large onion, chopped
1 medium potato, peeled and grated
1 medium carrot, peeled and grated
310 g (10 oz) canned bean mix, drained
1 egg, beaten
ground pepper to taste
1 tbsp Worcestershire sauce
$^1/_2$ cup tomato sauce

Makes 4 to 6 servings	
Kilojoules per serve	815
Calories per serve	195
Carbohydrate per serve	13 g
Fat	Negligible
Fibre	Excellent

1. Mix all ingredients together.

2. Line a baking dish with lightly greased foil. With wet hands shape meat mixture into a loaf on the foil. Cover with a second sheet of foil.

3. Bake in a moderately hot oven 190°C (375°F) for approximately 1 hour. Remove foil during final 20 minutes to brown if desired.

4. Leave to stand for 10–20 minutes before slicing.

ANN'S BEANY SHEPHERD'S PIE

440 g (14 oz) canned red kidney beans, drained
1 large onion, chopped
1 clove garlic, crushed
3 medium carrots, peeled and diced
1 medium capsicum, chopped
800 g (1 lb 9½ oz) canned peeled tomatoes
2 tbsp tomato paste
2 tsp mixed herbs
2 cups mashed potato (see Note)
½ cup grated low-fat cheese

Makes 6 servings	
Kilojoules per serve	575
Calories per serve	137
Carbohydrate per serve	16 g
Fat	Low
Fibre	Excellent

1. Combine beans, onion and garlic with other vegetables, tomato paste and herbs. Cook over low heat until liquid is reduced and mixture has thickened, for approximately 20 minutes.

2. Pour into a baking dish then top with mashed potato and grated cheese.

3. Bake in a hot oven 200°C (400°F) for 30 minutes or until topping is browned.

Note: For variation, substitute one cup of mashed pumpkin for one cup of mashed potato.

VEGETARIAN MOUSSAKA

1 large eggplant
2 tbsp salt
440 g (14 oz) canned red kidney beans, drained
1 large onion, chopped
1 clove garlic, crushed
425 g (13½ oz) canned peeled tomatoes, chopped
1 tbsp tomato paste
200 g (6½ oz) mushrooms, sliced
ground pepper to taste
½ tsp cinnamon

Makes 6 servings	
Kilojoules per serve	821
Calories per serve	196
Carbohydrate per serve	17 g
Fat	Low
Fibre	Excellent

1. Cut eggplant into slices, approximately 1 cm (½ in.) thick, then sprinkle with salt and leave to stand for 15–20 minutes. Rinse off salt then pat dry with paper towels.

2. Combine remaining ingredients.

3. Alternate layers of eggplant and bean mixture in a baking dish, ending with a layer of eggplant.

4. Cover with topping and grated cheese.

5. Bake in a moderately hot oven 190°C (375°F) for 30–40 minutes.

Topping
200 g (6½ oz) natural low-fat yoghurt
1 egg, beaten
ground pepper to taste
½ cup grated low-fat cheese

1. Combine yoghurt, egg and pepper together.

LENTIL CROQUETTES

1½ cups red lentils
3 cups water
1 large onion, peeled and finely chopped
½ tsp chilli powder
½ tsp mustard
½ tsp paprika
salt and ground pepper to taste
4 tbsp cottage cheese
1 cup wholemeal breadcrumbs

Makes 6 servings	
Kilojoules per serve	436
Calories per serve	104
Carbohydrate per serve	12 g
Fat	Negligible
Fibre	Excellent

1. Wash lentils well then cover with water. Bring to the boil then simmer gently for 20–30 minutes or until water has been absorbed (lentils should be quite dry).

2. Sauté onion in a non-stick pan with spices.

3. Mix together lentils, onion and spices, seasonings and cottage cheese.

4. Shape mixture into 12 croquettes then roll in breadcrumbs. Refrigerate for 10–20 minutes to 'set'.

5. Dry-fry croquettes in a non-stick pan, or alternatively bake in a moderately hot oven 190°C (375°F) for 25–30 minutes.

DUTCH-STYLE BAKED BEANS

1 packet (375 g/12 oz) cannellini or haricot beans
850 ml (28 fl oz) canned unsweetened tomato juice
1 medium onion, chopped
2 tbsp white vinegar
3 tbsp tomato paste
2 x 400 g (13 oz) canned peeled tomatoes
ground pepper to taste

Makes 4 to 6 servings	
Kilojoules per serve	575
Calories per serve	137
Carbohydrate per serve	23 g
Fat	Negligible
Fibre	Excellent

1. Soak beans in tomato juice overnight.

2. Place soaked beans, tomato juice, onion, vinegar, tomato paste, tomatoes and pepper in casserole dish.

3. Bake in a slow oven 150°C (300°F) for 3–4 hours or until beans are tender.

SLOPPY JOES

500 g (1 lb) lean minced steak
1 medium onion, chopped
1 clove garlic, crushed
salt and ground pepper to taste
440 g (14 oz) canned condensed tomato soup
440 g (14 oz) canned red kidney beans, drained
4 wholemeal hamburger buns

Makes 8 servings	
Kilojoules per serve	1162
Calories per serve	278
Carbohydrate per serve	27 g
Fat	Moderate
Fibre	Excellent

1. Brown mince with onion, garlic and seasonings in a non-stick pan.

2. Mix in tomato soup and beans and cook until heated through.

3. Toast buns then top each half with bean mixture.

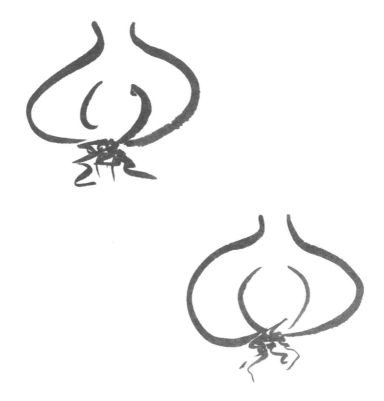

FISH AND SEAFOOD

Ask someone to tell you what their favourite restaurant cuisine is and more often than not they'll answer 'seafood'. We are blessed with a bountiful supply and variety of fish and seafood in Australia and gradually our fish consumption at home is increasing.

Fish and other seafood contain Omega-3 polyunsaturated fatty acids which, many research studies have now concluded, may lower the risk of heart disease and strokes if eaten regularly.

Fish and seafood are naturally low in fat and quick and easy to prepare. We've included cheaper fish types and canned fish to minimise expense.

PASTA WITH SMOKED SALMON

2 tsp olive oil
1 clove garlic, crushed
1 small onion, chopped
2 tbsp cornflour
$1^1/_2$ cups low-fat milk
pinch chicken stock powder
2 tbsp grated low-fat mozzarella cheese
$^1/_4$ cup finely chopped shallots (green onions)
1 tbsp drained capers
200 g ($6^1/_2$ oz) smoked salmon, cut into strips
400 g (13 oz) fettuccine or other pasta
ground black pepper and salt to taste
chopped fresh dill to garnish

Makes 4 servings	
Kilojoules per serve	656
Calories per serve	156
Carbohydrate per serve	9.7 g
Fat	Moderate
Fibre	Negligible

1. Heat olive oil in a saucepan over medium heat. Add garlic and onion and cook for 30 seconds.
2. Mix together cornflour and milk, then add to garlic and onion. Reduce heat to low and stir in stock powder. Cook over low heat until sauce bubbles and thickens. Add cheese and stir until cheese melts and sauce is smooth. Add shallots and capers.
3. Stir in smoked salmon.
4. Cook pasta in plenty of boiling water, following directions on the packet, then drain. Pour smoked salmon sauce over hot pasta.
5. Add pepper and salt to taste and garnish with dill.
6. Serve immediately with salad and crusty bread.

HEATWAVE CURRIED PRAWNS

500 g (1 lb) shelled prawns (see Note)
3 stalks celery, chopped
$^1/_4$ cup green olives, sliced
250 g (8 oz) natural low-fat yoghurt
1 tbsp tomato chutney
2 tsp lemon juice
2 tsp curry powder
2 cups cooked rice
$^1/_4$ cup low-joule French dressing
$^1/_3$ cup parsley, chopped

Makes 4 to 6 servings	
Kilojoules per serve	771
Calories per serve	184
Carbohydrate per serve	15 g
Fat	Low
Fibre	Good

1. Cut prawns into bite-sized pieces if necessary and combine with celery and olives.

2. Combine yoghurt, chutney, lemon juice and curry powder and pour over prawns.

3. Toss the rice in French dressing and parsley.

4. Line a salad bowl with the rice and fill centre with curried prawn mixture.

5. Serve well chilled with sliced cucumber and a green salad.

Note: To save expense substitute prawns with a 425 g (13$^1/_2$ oz) tin of tuna.

JAMAICAN FISH

1 large onion, thinly sliced

1 large red capsicum, sliced

425 g (13½ oz) canned tomatoes, drained and chopped

salt and ground pepper to taste

500 g (1 lb) fish fillets, boned and skinned

2 tbsp lemon juice

2 bananas, peeled and halved lengthwise

200 g (6½ oz) natural low-fat yoghurt

2 tbsp skim milk

2 cups wholemeal breadcrumbs

2 tbsp olive oil

Makes 4 to 6 servings	
Kilojoules per serve	1011
Calories per serve	242
Carbohydrate per serve	27 g
Fat	Low
Fibre	Excellent

1. Arrange half the onion, capsicum and tomatoes over the base of a shallow baking dish. Season to taste.

2. Place fish fillets over vegetables then sprinkle with lemon juice.

3. Place banana over fish.

4. Mix together yoghurt and skim milk then pour over fish.

5. Combine breadcrumbs and oil, and spoon over top layer.

6. Bake in a moderately hot oven 190°C (375°F) for 40 minutes. Serve with mashed potatoes and green peas.

FISH AU GRATIN

4 white fish fillets, such as ling
ground black pepper and salt to taste
300 ml (9½ fl oz) skim milk
3 tsp margarine
3 tsp plain flour
pinch mustard powder
100 g (3½ oz) low-fat cheddar cheese, grated
pinch ground paprika

Makes 4 servings	
Kilojoules per serve	931
Calories per serve	222
Carbohydrate per serve	7 g
Fat	Moderate
Fibre	Negligible

1. Season fish fillets with pepper and salt. Place in a flameproof casserole dish.

2. Pour milk over fish fillets, bring to the boil, then remove from heat. Cover and leave to infuse for 5 minutes.

3. Drain cooking liquid from fish into a saucepan.

4. Add margarine and flour to cooking liquid and, over a low heat, whisk continuously until sauce thickens. Cook for 1 minute.

5. Add mustard powder and half the cheese. Stir until cheese is melted.

6. Pour sauce over fish, sprinkle with paprika and remaining cheese.

7. Place under a preheated grill until golden brown.

8. Serve with steamed vegetables or wholemeal rolls and salad.

AMERICAN FISH PIE

1 large onion, chopped
2 tsp olive oil
1 cup frozen peas
2 cups frozen mixed vegetables
440 g (14 oz) canned cream of celery soup
425 g (13½ oz) canned Greenseas™ tuna or salmon, drained
2 cups mashed potato

Makes 4 servings	
Kilojoules per serve	1065
Calories per serve	254
Carbohydrate per serve	30 g
Fat	Low
Fibre	Excellent

1. Sauté onion in olive oil.
2. Combine remaining ingredients except potato with sautéed onion. Spoon mixture into baking dish.
3. Top with mashed potato.
4. Bake in a moderately hot oven 190°C (375°F) until potato topping is golden.
5. Serve with a crisp green salad.

EASY SALMON AND MUSHROOM SAVOURY

1 large onion, chopped
1 tbsp olive oil
1 small green capsicum, chopped
125 g (4 oz) mushrooms, sliced
440 g (14 oz) canned mushroom soup
1 cup water
1 bay leaf
pinch thyme
ground pepper to taste
440 g (14 oz) canned salmon, drained

Makes 4 servings	
Kilojoules per serve	911
Calories per serve	218
Carbohydrate per serve	6 g
Fat	Low
Fibre	Excellent

1. Sauté onion in oil, then add capsicum and mushrooms and cook until softened.
2. Stir in soup, water, bay leaf, thyme and pepper.
3. Add salmon then cook gently for 10 minutes or until heated through. Remove bay leaf.
4. Serve hot on a bed of rice with a crunchy coleslaw.

FILLETS PRINCESS

500 g (1 lb) fish fillets, boned and skinned
1 packet mushroom soup mix
6 shallots (green onions), finely chopped
440 g (14 oz) canned asparagus cuts, drained,
liquid reserved
¹/₂ cup white wine or water
ground pepper to taste

Makes 4 to 6 servings	
Kilojoules per serve	387
Calories per serve	92
Carbohydrate per serve	Negligible
Fat	Negligible
Fibre	Good

1. Arrange fish fillets over the base of a lightly greased baking dish.

2. Combine soup mix with shallots, reserved asparagus liquid, wine and pepper.

3. Pour over fish fillets then top with asparagus cuts.

4. Bake in a moderately hot oven 190°C (375°F) for 20–30 minutes.

5. Serve with jacket potatoes and green beans.

TUNA WHEAT CASSEROLE

1 cup cracked wheat (burghul) (see Note)

1¹/₂ cups hot water

1 medium onion, chopped

425 g (13¹/₂ oz) canned Greenseas™ tuna, drained and flaked

1 tbsp lemon juice

1 tbsp chopped parsley

¹/₂ cup green peas, cooked

ground pepper to taste

2 medium tomatoes, sliced

1 cup tomato juice

¹/₂ cup grated low-fat cheese

Makes 4 servings	
Kilojoules per serve	1431
Calories per serve	342
Carbohydrate per serve	30 g
Fat	Low
Fibre	Excellent

1. Place burghul in a lightly greased baking dish then pour over hot water. Leave to soak until all the water has been absorbed.

2. Top wheat with onion, tuna, lemon juice, parsley and peas. Season with pepper.

3. Arrange tomato slices over the top, pour over tomato juice then sprinkle evenly with grated cheese.

4. Bake in a moderately hot oven 190°C (375°F) for 30 minutes or until cheese is lightly browned and bubbly.

5. Serve with a tossed salad.

Note: If burghul is unavailable substitute with cooked brown rice.

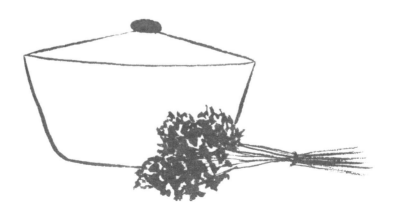

LAWRENCE'S GINGER SNAPPER

2 x 500 g (1 lb) whole snapper, cleaned

2 tbsp fresh root ginger, chopped

4–6 cups boiling water

2 tbsp soy sauce

4 shallots (green onions), finely chopped

Makes 4 servings	
Kilojoules per serve	800
Calories per serve	191
Carbohydrate per serve	Negligible
Fat	Low
Fibre	Negligible

1. Make three incisions diagonally along one side of each snapper, then insert two-thirds of the ginger.

2. Place remaining ginger in a wok filled with enough boiling water to cover the fish. Add soy sauce and bring to the boil.

3. Place fish in water and cook for 10–12 minutes or until flesh flakes. Then drain.

4. To serve place cooked fish on a heated platter and pour sauce over the top. Finish with chopped shallots.

5. Serve with steamed rice and stir-fried cabbage and baby corn.

Sauce

½ cup soy sauce

½ cup water

1 tbsp canola oil

1. Combine all ingredients. Simmer gently for 2 to 3 minutes.

MEDITERRANEAN FISH FRY

1 tbsp olive oil
1 medium onion, chopped
3 stalks celery, sliced
500 g (1 lb) fish fillets, boned, skinned and cut
into bite-sized pieces
2 cups broccoli florets, cooked
$^1/_2$ cup sticky raisins
$^1/_2$ tsp ground ginger
pinch cayenne pepper
ground pepper to taste
1 tbsp lemon juice

Makes 4 servings	
Kilojoules per serve	778
Calories per serve	186
Carbohydrate per serve	8 g
Fat	Low
Fibre	Excellent

1. Heat oil in a large frying pan. Sauté onion and celery until transparent.

2. Add remaining ingredients to pan and cook over a high heat until fish is just tender, stirring constantly.

3. Serve immediately on a bed of rice.

SEAFOOD CRISP

500 g (1 lb) marinara mix (see Note)
2 cups cooked macaroni or short pasta
1/2 cup grated low-fat cheese
125 g (4 oz) cottage cheese
1 medium onion, finely chopped
3 medium tomatoes, sliced
1/2 cup white wine or water
440 g (14 oz) canned cream of chicken soup
dash tabasco or chilli sauce
2 slices wholemeal bread
2 tsp reduced-fat margarine

Makes 4 servings	
Kilojoules per serve	1350
Calories per serve	323
Carbohydrate per serve	22 g
Fat	9 g
Fibre	Excellent

1. Layer marinara mix, pasta, half the grated cheese, cottage cheese, onion and tomatoes in a lightly greased baking dish.

2. Combine wine, soup and chilli sauce then pour over other ingredients.

3. Spread bread with margarine and cut into small cubes.

4. Top casserole with bread cubes and remaining grated cheese.

5. Bake in a hot oven 200°C (400°F) for 30–35 minutes or until topping is crisp and browned.

6. Serve with a salad.

Note: Marinara mix is available at fresh fish and seafood shops. If desired substitute with any tinned fish or cooked fish fillets.

TANIA'S TIPSY TROUT

3 cups water
3 cups dry white wine
1 medium carrot
1 medium onion
bouquet garni (thyme, parsley, bay leaf)
salt
peppercorns
1 medium (1.5 kg/3 lb) ocean trout, cleaned

Makes 4 servings	
Kilojoules per serve	1436
Calories per serve	344
Carbohydrate per serve	Negligible
Fat	Low
Fibre	Negligible

1. Combine water, wine, vegetables, herbs and seasonings in a large saucepan to form stock. Bring to the boil then simmer for 1 hour.

2. Place whole fish in a poaching pan, pour over cooled, strained stock. Cover and simmer for 15–20 minutes or until fish is cooked.

3. Serve whole on a platter either hot or cold, accompanied by whole steamed baby potatoes, cucumber sliced thickly and dressed with light mayonnaise or sour cream, and a sprinkling of paprika and fresh dill.

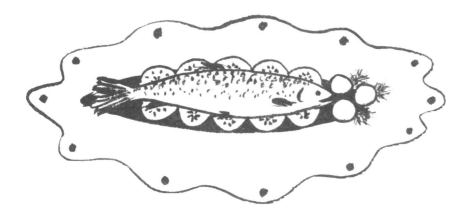

CHICKEN

Less than a decade ago, chicken was generally served only on 'special occasions' and at Christmas time. Today most families choose to eat chicken in some form at least one or more times per week. Nutritionally, chicken compares favourably with red meat in that they are both low in fat (if prepared appropriately without adding fat or oil), rich in high-quality protein, and loaded with minerals and vitamins.

We hope you enjoy our recipes which we have chosen because of their international flair, ease of preparation, and because we believe they will suit a wide variety of tastes.

JANICE'S GREEN CHICKEN CURRY

2 tbsp finely chopped root ginger
$^1/_2$ tbsp fresh chilli, finely chopped
6–8 cloves garlic, finely chopped
1 large onion, chopped
2 tsp olive oil
1 cup coconut cream
1$^1/_2$ cups canned evaporated skim milk
2 tbsp tomato paste
1 kg (2 lb) chicken breast fillets, sliced thinly
1 bunch fresh basil, chopped

Makes 6 to 8 servings	
Kilojoules per serve	1562
Calories per serve	373
Carbohydrate per serve	16 g
Fat	Moderate
Fibre	Negligible

1. Blend ginger, chilli, garlic and onion to a smooth paste in a food processor or blender.

2. Heat oil in a large heavy-based saucepan, add ginger mixture then cook over a low heat for 10 minutes—do not brown. Stir continuously.

3. Pour in coconut cream, evaporated milk and tomato paste. Bring to the boil then reduce heat to a gentle simmer. The curry flavour is improved if sauce is made the day before serving.

4. Add chicken and continue to cook over a low heat uncovered for 1 hour.

5. Stir in basil just before serving.

6. Serve with rice and yoghurt, chopped cucumber, banana and coconut, and pappadums.

Note: Pappadums can be microwaved on HIGH setting (2 minutes for 3 large pappadums).

CHICKEN AND ALMOND STIR FRY

400 g (13 oz) skinless chicken breast or thigh
fillets, cut into thin strips

2 tbsp plum sauce

2 tsp soy sauce

500 g (1 lb) Hokkien noodles

1 tbsp peanut oil

1 clove garlic, crushed

1 medium onion, sliced

200 g (6^1/$_2$ oz) broccoli florets

1 tsp cornflour

1 vegetable or chicken stock cube

^{1}/$_2$ cup water

^{1}/$_4$ cup toasted almonds

Makes 4 servings	
Kilojoules per serve	1695
Calories per serve	404
Carbohydrate per serve	40 g
Fat	Moderate
Fibre	Good

1. Place chicken in a baking dish and cover with plum sauce and soy sauce. Cover and allow to marinate overnight in the refrigerator.

2. Put noodles in a large bowl. Cover with boiling water and leave to heat through and soften, about 5 minutes. Drain, then rinse in cold water.

3. Heat oil in a wok over medium heat. Drain marinade from chicken and reserve. Stir fry chicken until cooked, remove from wok and set aside.

4. Add garlic and onion to wok and stir fry until soft.

5. Add broccoli and stir fry for 1 minute.

6. Mix cornflour and crumbled stock cube with water.

7. Add noodles, reserved marinade and cornflour mixture to wok. Stir until mixture boils and thickens slightly.

8. Stir in almonds and chicken. Heat through and serve.

LEMON CHICKEN

¹/₄ medium onion, peeled
1 x 1.5 kg (3 lb) chicken
salt and pepper to taste
¹/₄ tsp paprika
1 orange, juice and rind
¹/₂ lemon, juice and rind
¹/₂ cup pineapple juice
1 tbsp soy sauce

Makes 4 to 6 servings	
Kilojoules per serve	3409
Calories per serve	814
Carbohydrate per serve	3 g
Fat	8 g
Fibre	Negligible

1. Place onion inside chicken cavity.

2. Season cavity and skin with salt and pepper.

3. Sprinkle chicken with paprika, then place in a roasting dish, breast-side down.

4. Place orange and lemon rind inside chicken.

5. Combine orange, lemon and pineapple juice with soy sauce and pour over chicken.

6. Bake in a moderately hot oven 190°–200°C (375°–400°F) for 1¹/₂ hours, basting frequently. Turn chicken breast-side up after one hour.

7. Serve with baked potatoes, grilled tomatoes and zucchinis.

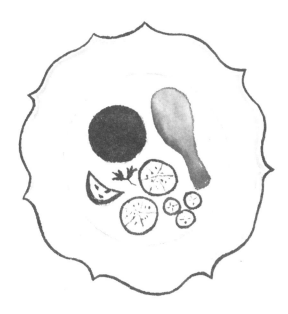

BAKED SPICY CHICKEN

4 chicken thigh fillets, skin and fat removed

1. Place chicken thighs in a baking dish.

Marinade
¹/₂ cup natural low-fat yoghurt
1 tsp lemon juice
1 clove garlic, crushed
¹/₂ tsp ground black pepper
¹/₂ tsp French mustard
¹/₄ tsp fresh ginger, grated

Makes 4 servings	
Kilojoules per serve	844
Calories per serve	201
Carbohydrate per serve	8 g
Fat	Low
Fibre	Negligible

1. Mix marinade ingredients together, then pour over chicken. Cover and allow to marinate overnight in the refrigerator.

Crumble
2 slices wholemeal bread
1 tbsp grated parmesan cheese

1. Tear bread into small pieces and mix with parmesan cheese.

2. Sprinkle crumble mixture over chicken.

3. Bake in a moderate oven 180°C (350°F) for about 45 minutes, or until chicken is cooked.

4. Serve with salad and potatoes in their jackets.

SUPERB POTATO CHICKEN

6 medium potatoes
$^1/_2$ cup chopped lean bacon or ham
1 medium onion, chopped
1 tsp sage
1 tbsp parsley, chopped
salt and ground pepper to taste
1 egg yolk
1.5 kg (3 lb) chicken
1 tbsp oil

Makes 4 to 6 servings	
Kilojoules per serve	2015
Calories per serve	482
Carbohydrate per serve	22 g
Fat	Moderate
Fibre	Good

1. Peel, cook and mash potatoes.

2. Mix together bacon, onion, potato, herbs, seasonings and egg yolk.

3. Place as much mixture under the chicken skin as possible and the remainder in the cavity. Tie or skewer legs together.

4. Brush chicken with oil and bake in a moderate oven 180°C (350°F) for 1$^1/_2$ hours.

5. Serve hot or cold with green beans and corn cobs.

TOMATO CHICKEN CASSEROLE

1.5 kg (3 lb) chicken pieces
1 cup plain flour seasoned with salt and pepper
1 tbsp olive oil
1 medium onion, chopped
1 clove garlic, crushed
$^1/_2$ tsp thyme
425 g (13$^1/_2$ oz) canned tomatoes, drained
125 g (4 oz) mushrooms, sliced
1 cup white wine
2 chicken stock cubes
salt and ground pepper to taste
1 bay leaf

Makes 4 to 6 servings	
Kilojoules per serve	1768
Calories per serve	420
Carbohydrate per serve	4 g
Fat	Moderate
Fibre	Negligible

1. Toss chicken pieces in seasoned flour.

2. Brown in hot oil.

3. Add onion and garlic to the pan to sauté.

4. Transfer chicken and onion into a baking dish.

5. Add remaining ingredients. Cover and bake in a moderate oven 180°C (350°F) for 1 hour.

6. Remove bay leaf before serving with steamed potatoes and spinach.

SPICY CHICKEN WINGS

¹/₄ cup tomato sauce
2 tbsp Worcestershire sauce
¹/₂ tsp black pepper
12 chicken wings

Makes 6 servings	
Kilojoules per serve	783
Calories per serve	187
Carbohydrate per serve	5 g
Fat	Moderate
Fibre	Negligible

1. Mix sauces together with pepper.

2. Pour over chicken wings in a baking dish.

3. Bake in a moderately hot oven 190°C (375°F) for 20–30 minutes or until tender. Alternatively, barbecue or microwave on HIGH for 5–10 minutes.

4. Serve with steamed rice and stir-fried vegetables.

WARM CHICKEN AND MINT SALAD

1 tsp canola oil
400 g (13 oz) skinless chicken breast or thigh fillets, chopped into bite-sized pieces
1 small red onion, thinly sliced
¹/₂ green capsicum, thinly sliced
1 cup lettuce leaves, roughly torn
¹/₂ cup mint leaves

Makes 4 servings	
Kilojoules per serve	662
Calories per serve	158
Carbohydrate per serve	3.5 g
Fat	Low
Fibre	Negligible

1. Heat oil in a wok over a medium heat. Add chicken and stir fry until cooked. Remove from wok and set aside.

2. In a large bowl, toss together chicken, onion, capsicum, lettuce and mint leaves.

Dressing
1 tbsp light soy sauce
¹/₂ tbsp fish sauce
3 tbsp lemon or lime juice
1 clove garlic, crushed
¹/₂ tsp grated ginger
2 tsp olive oil
1 tbsp sweet chilli sauce

1. Put all ingredients for dressing in a small jar and shake well.

2. Pour over salad. Toss lightly and serve with crusty bread.

STOVE-TOP CHICKEN DINNER

1 kg (2 lb) chicken pieces
$^1/_2$ lemon, squeezed
$^1/_2$ cup orange juice
salt and ground pepper to taste
1 tsp crushed rosemary leaves
$^1/_2$ cup water
4 medium new potatoes, washed
6 small carrots, scraped
2 tbsp cornflour
1 cup evaporated skim milk
parsley, chopped

Makes 4 to 6 servings	
Kilojoules per serve	753
Calories per serve	180
Carbohydrate per serve	27 g
Fat	Low
Fibre	Good

1. Place chicken pieces in a heavy-based saucepan. Add juices, seasonings, rosemary, water and vegetables.

2. Cover and bring to the boil then reduce heat and simmer for approximately 45 minutes or until chicken and vegetables are tender.

3. Blend cornflour with evaporated skim milk then pour into casserole and stir until thickened.

4. Serve garnished with chopped parsley.

HOME-MADE CHICKEN NUGGETS

375 g (12 oz) boneless chicken fillets, skinned
2 tbsp natural low-fat yoghurt
$1/2$ cup breadcrumbs, toasted
1 tbsp parmesan cheese
$1/2$ tsp mixed herbs

Makes 4 to 6 servings	
Kilojoules per serve	768
Calories per serve	184
Carbohydrate per serve	10 g
Fat	Moderate
Fibre	Good

1. Cut chicken fillets into large bite-sized pieces then place in a bowl.

2. Stir in yoghurt to coat chicken pieces evenly.

3. In a shallow dish combine crumbs, cheese and herbs.

4. Toss chicken in crumbs until well covered.

5. Place in a lightly greased baking dish, and bake in a moderately hot oven 190°C (375°F) for 25 minutes or until lightly browned.

6. Serve hot with dipping sauce and oven-fried chips.

Sauce
100 g ($3^1/2$ oz) natural low-fat yoghurt
1 tsp soy sauce
1 tbsp tomato sauce
$1/4$ –$1/2$ tsp minced garlic
1 tbsp finely chopped celery
freshly ground black pepper to taste

1. Combine all ingredients.

2. Chill for 30 minutes before serving.

BEEF, LAMB AND PORK

Whether you prefer lamb or beef or pork, our recipes will surely please you with their interesting, sometimes unusual, combinations and ingredients.

We've minimised fat content and lengthy preparation, and have chosen recipes that are not only our favourites, but we believe are suitable for entertaining or just enjoying with the family.

SIMA'S CABBAGE ROLLS

1 large savoy cabbage
1 tbsp whole cloves
1 tbsp black peppercorns
$^1/_2$ cup white vinegar
500 g (1 lb) lean minced steak or veal
2 large onions, finely chopped
$2^1/_2$ cups cooked rice
salt and ground pepper to taste
2 cups tomato sauce
2 cups tomato juice
1 cup red wine or stock

Makes 6 to 8 servings	
Kilojoules per serve	1323
Calories per serve	315
Carbohydrate per serve	40 g
Fat	Low
Fibre	Excellent

1. Place cabbage, cloves, peppercorns and vinegar in a large saucepan.

2. Cover with water. Bring to the boil then simmer for 1 hour.

3. Drain in colander for 1 hour or longer, then carefully separate leaves.

4. Mix together mince, onions, rice and seasonings.

5. Divide meat mixture evenly among 12–16 cabbage leaves.

6. Roll up neatly then place seam-side down in a large baking dish.

7. Combine tomato sauce, juice and wine, then pour over rolls.

8. Bake in a moderate oven 180°C (350°F) for 1–1$^1/_2$ hours.

9. Serve with light sour cream or yoghurt.

VIRGINIA-STYLE CORNED BEEF

2 kg (4 lb) corned silverside
2 tbsp vinegar
1 tsp whole cloves
2 tbsp brown sugar
$^1/_2$ cup soft breadcrumbs
$^1/_4$ tsp dry mustard
1 tbsp orange rind, grated
2 tsp lemon rind, grated
$^1/_4$ cup orange juice
1 tbsp lemon juice
$^1/_2$ cup apple juice

Makes 6 to 8 servings	
Kilojoules per serve	1221
Calories per serve	292
Carbohydrate per serve	6 g
Fat	Moderate
Fibre	Negligible

1. Place corned silverside in a large saucepan with vinegar. Cover with water and bring to the boil, then reduce heat and simmer for 3 hours or until tender.

2. Cool, then refrigerate in cooking liquid overnight.

3. Drain meat then stud with cloves.

4. Mix together sugar, breadcrumbs, mustard, and orange and lemon rind, then pat firmly onto meat.

5. Place in a foil-lined baking dish and bake in a hot oven 230°C (450°F) for 10 minutes.

6. Reduce heat to moderate 180°C (350°F) and continue to bake for 1 hour, basting with combined orange, lemon and apple juice.

7. Serve sliced hot or cold with parsley potatoes, carrots and cabbage.

SWEET AND SOUR MEATBALLS

$^1/_2$ cup soft breadcrumbs

1 onion, chopped

1 tsp salt

1 tsp pepper

$^3/_4$ cup water

1 kg (2 lb) minced topside steak

2 tbsp chopped parsley

2 tsp sugar

3 tsp ground ginger

2 tsp soy sauce

1 egg, lightly beaten

1 tbsp vegetable oil

$^3/_4$ cup water

1 stock cube

Makes 6 servings	
Kilojoules per serve	1027
Calories per serve	245
Carbohydrate per serve	20 g
Fat	Moderate
Fibre	Excellent

1. Combine breadcrumbs, onion, salt, pepper and water, and let stand for a few minutes.

2. Add the minced steak, parsley, sugar, ginger, soy sauce and egg. Mix well.

3. Shape into balls, heat oil in a non-stick pan and brown meatballs. Remove meatballs from pan and pour off any remaining oil.

4. Add water and stock cube, bring to boiling point and add meatballs. Cover and simmer for approximately 20 minutes. Pour liquid off meatballs and discard.

5. Pour over Sweet and Sour Vegetable Sauce (see page 34) and heat through.

6. Serve with fluffy boiled rice.

ITALIAN BEEF ROLL

1 kg (2 lb) piece rump or topside steak
125 g (4 oz) minced veal
$^{1}/_{2}$ cup soft breadcrumbs
2 tbsp parmesan cheese
freshly ground black pepper
1 tsp oregano
60 g (2 oz) Italian salami, cut into julienne strips
60 g (2 oz) low-fat mozzarella cheese, cut into strips
425 g (13$^{1}/_{2}$ oz) canned tomato purée
2 tbsp tomato paste
1 medium onion, chopped
2 cloves garlic, crushed
$^{1}/_{3}$ cup red wine

Makes 4 to 6 servings	
Kilojoules per serve	1194
Calories per serve	284
Carbohydrate per serve	7 g
Fat	Moderate
Fibre	Good

1. Butterfly the steak then pound until thin.

2. Combine veal, breadcrumbs, parmesan, pepper and oregano, then spread mixture evenly over the steak.

3. Top with salami and cheese strips then roll up and secure with string.

4. Brown evenly in a non-stick pan. Transfer to a baking dish.

5. Combine tomato purée, tomato paste, onion, garlic and red wine.

6. Bake in a moderate oven 180°C (350°F) for 30 minutes. Alternatively microwave on HIGH for 8–10 minutes.

7. Serve hot, sliced, and with sauce spooned over meat, accompanied with a salad and crusty Italian rolls.

LENTIL-STUFFED PORK

Recipe courtesy of the Australian Pork Corporation

6 pork steaks
$^1/_2$ cup red lentils, rinsed
2 tbsp finely chopped onion
$^2/_3$ cup diced pumpkin
1 cup chicken stock or water
1 tsp curry powder
1 egg white
$1^1/_2$ tbsp flaked almonds, toasted

Makes 6 servings	
Kilojoules per serve	906
Calories per serve	216
Carbohydrate per serve	3 g
Fat	Low
Fibre	Good

1. Cut pockets in each steak with a sharp knife.

2. Place lentils, onion, pumpkin, stock and curry powder in a saucepan. Simmer gently until the liquid has evaporated, for approximately 15 minutes. Mash until smooth.

3. Whip egg white until stiff, then fold lightly into lentil mix with half the nuts.

4. Spoon two-thirds of mixture into steaks.

5. Grill each side for approximately 5 minutes, then spoon over remaining lentil mixture and sprinkle with rest of nuts.

6. Place back under grill at a reduced heat until topping is set and reheated.

7. Serve with jacket potatoes and a tossed salad.

LAMB WITH GARLIC AND ROSEMARY

1.5 kg (3 lb) half leg of lamb
2 large cloves garlic, cut into slivers
large sprig of fresh rosemary
olive oil
black pepper

Makes 6 to 8 servings	
Kilojoules per serve	738
Calories per serve	176
Carbohydrate per serve	Nil
Fat	Low
Fibre	Nil

1. Pierce the meat with a sharp knife in several places, and insert the garlic slivers.

2. Push the sprig of rosemary into the centre of the lamb.

3. Rub a little oil over the meat and season with black pepper.

4. Place meat in a moderately hot oven 190°C (375°F) and roast for 1¹/₂ hours.

5. Serve with jacket potatoes and minted peas.

JILL'S CRUSTY LAMB

1.5 kg (3 lb) leg of lamb
1 egg, beaten
30 g (1 oz) margarine, melted
1$^1/_2$ cups soft wholemeal breadcrumbs
1 tbsp sesame seeds
$^1/_2$ tsp salt
$^1/_2$ tsp marjoram
1 small onion, sliced

Makes 6 to 8 servings	
Kilojoules per serve	1093
Calories per serve	260
Carbohydrate per serve	8 g
Fat	Moderate
Fibre	Negligible

1. Brush lamb with beaten egg, then place into a greased baking dish. Reserve 1 tablespoon beaten egg.

2. Combine margarine, breadcrumbs, sesame seeds, salt and marjoram.

3. Mix in remaining egg.

4. Press mixture over lamb, then press onion rings into seasoning mixture.

5. Bake in a moderate oven 180°C (350°F) for 1$^1/_2$ hours or until meat is cooked. Cover crust with foil when it is crisp to prevent over-browning.

6. Serve with baked sweet potato, spinach and tomato sauté.

LAMB STEAKS ORIENTAL

4 lamb steaks

$1/4$ tsp ground ginger

2 tsp brown sugar

$1/2$ tsp garlic salt

2 tsp soy sauce

2 tsp sherry

1 tsp olive oil

1 large onion, sliced into thin wedges

2 stalks celery, sliced

1 capsicum, sliced

1 tbsp cornflour

$1/2$ cup water

Makes 4 servings	
Kilojoules per serve	1181
Calories per serve	282
Carbohydrate per serve	7 g
Fat	Moderate
Fibre	Good

1. Trim fat from steaks then snip edges to prevent curling.

2. Mix together ginger, sugar, garlic salt, soy sauce and sherry in a shallow dish. Marinate lamb in mixture while preparing vegetables.

3. Heat oil then sauté onion, celery and capsicum until soft.

4. Add cornflour to vegetables then pour in water mixed with the marinade poured off the lamb. Stir until boiling.

5. Pat lamb steaks dry then either grill or dry fry.

6. Pour sauce over steaks and serve with rice.

PASTA AND PIES

Many of us choose to eat less meat-, fish- and poultry-based meals these days. We have become more health conscious and concerned about our intake of saturated fat and cholesterol. Not surprisingly, cooked breakfasts of lambs' fry and bacon, and traditional roast dinners are becoming less frequent than they were in the past.

The Commonwealth Department of Health Dietary Guidelines for Australians state that we should eat more breads, cereals, whole grains, fruits and vegetables as part of a healthy diet. As a result of this well-publicised health message, meals based on rice, pasta and vegetables are becoming more and more popular, as well as nutritionally important.

SPINACH AND PARSLEY FETTUCCINE

2 tbsp pine nuts
400 g (13 oz) spinach fettuccine
2 tsp olive oil
1 medium onion, sliced finely
2 cloves garlic, crushed
1 packet (250 g/8 oz) frozen spinach
1 cup chopped parsley
1 tbsp grated parmesan cheese

Makes 4 servings	
Spinach Parsley Sauce:	
Kilojoules per serve	241
Calories per serve	57
Carbohydrate per serve	Negligible
Fat	Low
Fibre	Good

1. Toast pine nuts in a non-stick frying pan on low heat for 3–4 minutes, shaking often, until golden brown. Do not allow to burn.

2. Cook fettuccine in boiling water, following directions on the packet, then drain.

3. Heat oil in a non-stick frying pan over low heat. Add onion and garlic and cook so onion sweats and softens without browning.

4. Add spinach and stir until it thaws and is hot. Add parsley and stir in well.

5. Pour sauce over fettuccine and mix well. Transfer to four individual pasta bowls.

6. Sprinkle each serving with toasted pine nuts and parmesan cheese, and serve.

CREAMY PORK 'N' PASTA

500 g (1 lb) lean pork steaks
2 tsp olive oil
250 g (8 oz) mushrooms, sliced
500 g (1 lb) fettuccine
250 g (8 oz) ricotta cheese
1/4 cup fresh basil leaves, chopped
ground black pepper to taste
2 tbsp grated parmesan cheese

Makes 4 servings	
Kilojoules per serve	1335
Calories per serve	320
Carbohydrate per serve	23 g
Fat	Low
Fibre	Good

1. Cut pork steaks into thin strips. Sauté in oil until lightly browned, then add mushrooms and cook for 4–5 minutes or until mushrooms have softened.

2. Cook fettuccine as directed on packet. Drain and reserve 1/3–1/2 cup of cooking water.

3. Beat ricotta with a wooden spoon until smooth. Add reserved cooking water and blend to desired sauce consistency in a saucepan.

4. Combine cooked pasta, pork, mushrooms, and ricotta in a saucepan. Stir in basil and pepper to taste then heat through gently.

5. Serve sprinkled with parmesan cheese.

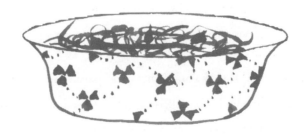

TURKEY TETRAZZINI

250 g (8 oz) fettuccine
1$\frac{1}{2}$ cups canned evaporated skim milk
1 tbsp cornflour
1$\frac{1}{2}$ cups broccoli florets, cooked and drained
1 cup mushrooms, sliced
2 shallots (green onions), chopped
500 g (1 lb) cooked turkey, sliced into strips
salt and ground pepper to taste
2 tbsp grated parmesan cheese

Makes 4 to 6 servings	
Kilojoules per serve	1101
Calories per serve	263
Carbohydrate per serve	22 g
Fat	Low
Fibre	Excellent

1. Cook fettuccine as directed on packet.

2. Combine skim milk with cornflour and cook over a low heat until thickened.

3. Stir in broccoli, mushrooms, shallots, turkey and seasonings to taste.

4. Add cooked fettuccine then pour in a serving dish.

5. Sprinkle with parmesan cheese.

OUR FAVOURITE SPAGHETTI BOLOGNAISE SAUCE

500 g (1 lb) minced veal
1 medium onion, chopped
1 clove garlic, crushed
425 g (13$\frac{1}{2}$ oz) canned tomatoes, chopped, with liquid
4 tbsp tomato paste
$\frac{1}{2}$ cup tomato sauce
2 tsp oregano
2 tsp basil
$\frac{1}{2}$ cup red wine
salt and ground pepper to taste

Makes 4 to 6 servings	
Kilojoules per serve	533
Calories per serve	127
Carbohydrate per serve	5 g
Fat	Low
Fibre	Negligible

1. Brown veal with onion and garlic in a non-stick pan.

2. Stir in tomatoes, tomato paste, sauce, herbs, wine and seasonings.

3. Simmer over a low heat for 30–40 minutes (or longer, to develop flavour).

SHEENA'S FETTUCCINE WITH PRAWNS AND SNOW PEAS

500 g (1 lb) green prawns, shelled
1 cup dry white wine
1 small onion, finely chopped
1 tsp olive oil
500 g (1 lb) mixed tomato, spinach and plain
fettuccine
2 tbsp grated parmesan cheese
200 ml (6½ fl oz) cream
10 snow peas, topped, tailed and cut into thick strips
ground pepper to taste

Makes 4 to 6 servings	
Kilojoules per serve	1641
Calories per serve	393
Carbohydrate per serve	33 g
Fat	Low
Fibre	Good

1. Simmer prawns in wine for 3–5 minutes. Drain.

2. Sauté onion in olive oil, add prawns and wine, then remove from heat.

3. Cook fettuccine in boiling water as directed on packet, drain, then return to saucepan.

4. Stir parmesan through cooked pasta. Keep hot.

5. Pour cream over prawns and onion, and heat gently—do not boil.

6. Add cream mixture and snow peas to pasta. Season to taste.

7. Serve immediately with a green salad and crusty bread.

CLAIRE'S SPINACH AND THREE-CHEESE CANNELLONI

Base

2 tsp olive oil

1 onion, chopped

1 clove garlic, crushed

425 g (13$^1/_2$ oz) canned peeled tomatoes, chopped

2 tbsp tomato paste

$^1/_4$ cup red wine

1 tsp dried basil

1 tbsp chopped continental parsley

1 bay leaf

ground black pepper to taste

Makes 6 servings	
Kilojoules per serve	1074
Calories per serve	257
Carbohydrate per serve	19 g
Fat	Low
Fibre	Good

1. Heat oil then sauté onion and garlic.

2. Add remaining ingredients and simmer for 20 minutes.

3. Remove bay leaf. Set base mixture aside.

Sauce

2 tbsp margarine

2 tbsp plain flour

2 cups skim milk

$^1/_4$ cup freshly grated parmesan cheese

1. While base is simmering, melt margarine in a small saucepan over moderate heat.

2. Add flour and stir until smooth. Add milk gradually, stirring constantly until sauce boils and thickens.

3. Stir in parmesan cheese, then set aside.

Filling

1 packet (250 g/8 oz) frozen spinach, thawed and drained

250 g (8 oz) ricotta cheese

$^1/_4$ cup grated parmesan cheese

$^1/_2$ tsp nutmeg

freshly ground black pepper to taste

250 g (8 oz) cannelloni tubes

1. Combine all ingredients except cannelloni tubes, mixing well to blend.

2. Place filling into a piping bag then fill each cannelloni tube.

Topping
2 tbsp grated low-fat cheese
1 tbsp cornflake crumbs

1. To assemble the dish, pour base mixture into a shallow ovenproof dish.

2. Arrange cannelloni on top then pour cheese sauce over tubes so they are completely covered.

3. Sprinkle with topping.

4. Bake in a moderate oven 180°C (350°F) for 30 minutes or until tubes are soft.

TASTY VEGETABLE PIE

Base

¹/₂ cup Kellogg's All-Bran™

¹/₄ cup skim milk

2 tbsp margarine

³/₄ cup self-raising flour

Makes 6 servings

Kilojoules per serve	1170
Calories per serve	279
Carbohydrate per serve	28 g
Fat	Moderate
Fibre	Excellent

1. Soak All-Bran™ in milk for 5 minutes. Rub margarine through flour with fingertips then mix in bran mixture to form a stiff dough.

2. Roll out to a circle 1 cm (¹/₂ in.) thick, then press over the base and sides of 20 cm (8 in.) pie plate.

Filling

3 cups soft, cooked vegetables (see Note)

3 tbsp tomato sauce

¹/₂ tsp mixed herbs

4 tbsp cottage cheese

salt and ground pepper to taste

1. Mix vegetables together with sauce, herbs, cottage cheese and salt and pepper. Spoon mixture over pastry.

Topping

3 tbsp wholemeal breadcrumbs

2 tsp sesame seeds

3 tbsp parmesan cheese

2 tsp poppy seeds

1. Combine all ingredients then sprinkle evenly over the top of vegetables.

2. Bake in a hot oven 200°C (400°F) for 30–40 minutes or until pastry crust is lightly browned and crisp.

Note: Potato, pumpkin, carrot and peas are a good combination for this pie.

SPEEDY MEXICAN PIZZA

4 wholemeal pita bread pockets
4 tbsp tomato paste
440 g (14 oz) canned red kidney beans
$^{1}/_{4}$ tsp chilli powder (optional)
1 medium onion, finely chopped
1 large capsicum, finely chopped
1 large tomato, finely chopped
$^{1}/_{2}$ cup grated low-fat tasty cheese

Makes 4 servings	
Kilojoules per serve	1088
Calories per serve	260
Carbohydrate per serve	34 g
Fat	Low
Fibre	Excellent

1. Spread bread with tomato paste.

2. Drain beans and mash roughly with a fork.

3. Spread over bread, sprinkle with chilli powder.

4. Top with onion, capsicum, tomato and lastly, cheese.

5. Bake in a hot oven 200°C (400°F) for 15–20 minutes or until cheese is melted and bubbly.

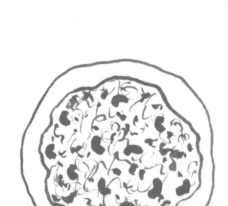

ASPARAGUS RICE FLAN

Base

2 cups cooked brown rice

1 egg, beaten

$^1/_2$ tsp mixed herbs

440 g (14 oz) canned asparagus cuts, drained

Makes 6 servings	
Kilojoules per serve	971
Calories per serve	232
Carbohydrate per serve	14 g
Fat	Low
Fibre	Good

1. Mix rice, egg and herbs together then press into bottom and sides of a greased pie plate.

2. Arrange asparagus over base.

Filling

2 eggs

500 g (1 lb) cottage cheese

pinch of cayenne pepper

1 tbsp parmesan cheese

1. Combine eggs, cottage cheese and pepper in a blender or food processor. Blend until smooth then pour over base and sprinkle with parmesan cheese.

2. Bake in a hot oven 200°C (400°F) for 20–30 minutes until set and golden.

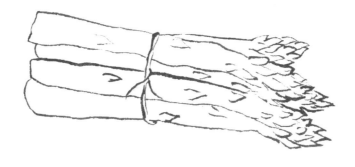

SALMON QUICHE

Base

1 tbsp margarine
1 tsp oil
1 cup plain, wholemeal flour
$^1/_2$ cup skim milk

Makes 6 servings

Kilojoules per serve	1737
Calories per serve	415
Carbohydrate per serve	25 g
Fat	Moderate
Fibre	Excellent

1. Rub margarine and oil through flour with fingertips. Add enough milk to make a stiff, sticky dough.

2. Roll out dough into a circle 1 cm ($^1/_2$ in.) thick, then line base and sides of a 20 cm (8 in.) quiche or flan dish.

3. Bake in a hot oven 220°C (425°F) for 10 minutes.

Filling

3 silverbeet leaves, trimmed and chopped
1 small onion, finely chopped
210 g (7 oz) canned salmon, drained
500 g (1 lb) cottage cheese
2 tbsp natural low-fat yoghurt
2 eggs, beaten
$^1/_2$ cup plain, wholemeal flour
salt and ground pepper to taste
$^3/_4$ cup grated low-fat cheese

1. Steam or microwave silverbeet until soft.

2. Combine silverbeet with onion, salmon, cottage cheese, yoghurt, eggs, flour, seasonings and half the grated cheese. Pour over cooked base.

3. Sprinkle with remaining cheese then bake in a hot oven 220°C (425°F) for 30 minutes or until set.

DESSERTS AND SWEETS

Having a sweet tooth is nothing to be ashamed of or feel guilty about. Keeping the fat and added sugar content down means our dessert recipes are quite healthy and, we think, a delightful way to end a meal.

Please note we have included a small amount of sugar in our recipes since this improves their appearance and taste. This should not have any effect on your blood sugar levels. Enjoy!

LINDY'S APPLE CRUMBLE

4 cooking apples
3 whole cloves
$^1/_2$ cup orange juice
$^1/_2$ cup plain, wholemeal flour
1 cup rolled oats
$^1/_4$ cup wheat germ
$^1/_4$ cup raw sugar
3 tbsp margarine

Makes 8 to 10 servings	
Kilojoules per serve	653
Calories per serve	156
Carbohydrate per serve	23 g
Fat	Low
Fibre	Excellent

1. Peel, core and slice apples.

2. Place in ovenproof dish. Add cloves and pour over orange juice.

3. Place flour, rolled oats, wheat germ and sugar in a mixing bowl and rub in margarine until mixture is crumbly.

4. Spread crumble mixture evenly over apples and bake in a moderate oven 180°C (350°F) for 1 hour or until topping is crisp and browned.

RICE PUDDING CAKE

2 cups cooked rice
3 eggs, beaten
2 medium, ripe bananas, mashed
2 apples, cored and finely chopped
300 g (9½ oz) cottage cheese
¼ cup sultanas
2 tbsp sugar (or artificial sweetener equivalent)
pinch each ground nutmeg and cinnamon
natural yoghurt to serve (optional)

Makes 12 servings	
Kilojoules per serve	415
Calories per serve	99
Carbohydrate per serve	14 g
Fat	Negligible
Fibre	Good

1. In large bowl, combine rice, eggs, bananas, apples, cottage cheese, sultanas and sugar. Mix well.

2. Turn into paper-lined and lightly greased 20 cm (8 in.) springform tin. Sprinkle with spices.

3. Bake in a hot oven 220°C (425°F) until firm and cooked through, for about 1 hour. Cool slightly in tin; remove to a serving plate. Carefully peel off paper. Cool completely.

4. Chill until served. Dollop servings with a little yoghurt if desired.

DATE AND RAISIN CHEESECAKE

Base

1 tbsp margarine

1 cup self-raising flour

$1/4$ cup rolled oats

$1/2$ tsp ground ginger

4–5 tbsp water

Makes 12 servings	
Kilojoules per serve	549
Calories per serve	131
Carbohydrate per serve	10 g
Fat	Low
Fibre	Good

1. In bowl, rub margarine into flour until crumbly. Mix in oats, ginger and enough of the water to make a stiff, dry dough.

2. Roll out dough to a circle, 1 cm ($1/2$ in.) thick. Carefully press into base of a greased 25 cm (10 in.) springform tin. Set aside.

Filling

1 kg (2 lb) ricotta cheese

4 eggs, lightly beaten

300 ml ($9^1/2$ fl oz) evaporated skim milk

$1/2$ cup raisins, chopped

1 tbsp grated lemon peel

2 tbsp sugar (or artificial sweetener equivalent)

1. Beat together cheese and eggs. Gradually beat in evaporated milk until smooth.

2. Stir in raisins, lemon peel and sugar. Pour mixture over prepared base.

3. Bake at 200°C (400°F) for 15 minutes. Reduce oven to 190°C (375°F). Continue baking for $1^1/4$–$1^1/2$ hours or until knife inserted in centre comes out clean. Cool on wire rack.

Topping

1 cup dates, pitted and chopped

$1/2$ cup unsweetened orange juice

1. In small saucepan, simmer dates in orange juice until reduced to a soft, pasty consistency. Cool.

2. Spread evenly over cooled cheesecake. Chill until served.

Note: Topping can be stored separately and spooned on to cheesecake at serving time if desired.

LEMON CUSTARD CHEESECAKE

Base

1 packet (250 g/8 oz) wheatmeal biscuits,
finely crushed
125 g (4 oz) margarine, melted
$^1/_2$ tsp nutmeg

Makes 6 to 8 servings	
Kilojoules per serve	805
Calories per serve	192
Carbohydrate per serve	17 g
Fat	Moderate
Fibre	Negligible

1. Combine biscuit crumbs with melted margarine, add nutmeg and mix well.

2. Press mixture firmly over base and sides of a deep 20 cm (8 in.) pie plate, then refrigerate while preparing filling.

Filling

1 packet low-joule lemon jelly crystals
$^1/_2$ cup boiling water
250 g (8 oz) cottage cheese, sieved
$^1/_2$ cup lemon juice
1$^1/_2$ cups cold thick custard (see Note)

1. Dissolve jelly crystals in boiling water, then cool.

2. Mix together cottage cheese and lemon juice. Gradually pour in cooled jelly mixture.

3. Fold in custard. Pour over crumb crust and chill to set.

Note: Use 3 tbsp custard powder and 1$^1/_2$ cups skim milk.

CREAMY RICE

3 cups skim milk

²/₃ cup short grain or Arborio rice

1¹/₂ tbsp sultanas

¹/₈ tsp ground cardamom

2¹/₂ tbsp unsalted pistachio nuts, chopped and toasted

Makes 6 servings	
Kilojoules per serve	754
Calories per serve	180
Carbohydrate per serve	29 g
Fat	Low
Fibre	Good

1. Place milk, rice and sultanas in a large saucepan.

2. Bring to the boil over medium heat, then reduce to simmer and cover.

3. Cook until mixture thickens, about 45 minutes, stirring occasionally.

4. Stir through cardamom.

5. Serve rice in individual bowls, topped with pistachio nuts.

OATY APPLES

4 granny smith apples, cored

³/₄ cup rolled oats

¹/₂ cup apple juice

¹/₂ cup sultanas

¹/₂ cup desiccated coconut

1 tsp mixed spice

Makes 4 servings	
Kilojoules per serve	923
Calories per serve	220
Carbohydrate per serve	39 g
Fat	Low
Fibre	Very good

1. Score skin around the centre of each apple then place in a baking dish.

2. Mix oats, juice, sultanas, coconut and spice. Press one quarter of this mixture firmly into each apple.

3. Bake in a hot oven 200°C (400°F) for 30 minutes.

4. Serve with custard, natural yoghurt or ice-cream.

RAYA'S APPLE AND APRICOT STRUDEL

Pastry

2 cups self-raising flour

2 tbsp margarine

2 tbsp skim milk

2 tbsp low-joule apricot jam

Makes 6 to 8 servings	
Kilojoules per serve	666
Calories per serve	159
Carbohydrate per serve	28 g
Fat	Low
Fibre	Very good

1. Sift flour into a basin. Rub in margarine with fingertips. Stir in milk to make a soft dough.

2. Turn onto a floured board and knead lightly. Roll out thinly to a rectangle 30 x 40 cm (12 x 16 in.), then spread with apricot jam.

Filling

2 apples, peeled, sliced and cooked

425 g (13$^{1}/_{2}$ oz) canned unsweetened apricots, drained

$^{1}/_{2}$ cup sultanas

2 tbsp soft breadcrumbs

1 tsp cinnamon

1 egg yolk, beaten

1. Spread apples, apricots, sultanas, breadcrumbs and cinnamon along long edge of pastry.

2. Roll up and place on a lightly greased oven tray, brush with beaten egg yolk. Score strudel diagonally with a sharp knife.

3. Bake in a moderately hot oven 190°C (375°F) for 45 minutes or until golden.

STRAWBERRY RICOTTA CUPS

Recipe courtesy of Searle Australia

2 punnets strawberries, sliced
2 tsp vanilla essence
6 sachets artificial sweetener (Equal™)
500 g (1 lb) ricotta cheese
400 g (13 oz) natural low-fat yoghurt
6 whole strawberries and mint sprigs to decorate

Makes 6 servings	
Kilojoules per serve	848
Calories per serve	203
Carbohydrate per serve	8 g
Fat	Low
Fibre	Good

1. Sprinkle strawberries with vanilla and three sachets of sweetener, then refrigerate for 30 minutes.

2. Beat or blend ricotta until smooth, then stir in yoghurt and remaining sweetener.

3. Spoon a layer of strawberries into individual serving dishes. Top with ricotta mixture, then decorate with strawberries and mint.

JUDY'S CUSTARD PLUMS

12 plums
4 tsp sugar (or artificial sweetener equivalent)
250 g (8 oz) cottage cheese
3 eggs
1/2 cup skim milk

Makes 4 servings	
Kilojoules per serve	706
Calories per serve	168
Carbohydrate per serve	15 g
Fat	Low
Fibre	Good

1. Halve and stone plums. Place in a heavy-based saucepan, then sprinkle with sugar and cook over a moderate heat until plums have softened and syrup darkened—for about 10 minutes.

2. Spoon three plum halves each into four individual ovenproof dishes.

3. Blend cottage cheese, eggs and milk. Pour this custard evenly over plums.

4. Bake in a water bath in a moderate oven 180°C (350°F) for 40 minutes or until custard has set.

CHOCOLATE MOUSSE

2 eggs, separated
1 1/2 cups evaporated skim milk
1 tbsp cocoa
3 1/2 tsp gelatine
3 tbsp hot water
3 sachets artificial sweetner (Equal™)
strawberries to decorate

Makes 6 servings	
Kilojoules per serve	195
Calories per serve	47
Carbohydrate per serve	7 g
Fat	Low
Fibre	Negligible

1. Beat egg yolks and place in a saucepan with milk and cocoa.

2. Stirring constantly, warm the mixture over medium heat, being careful not to boil. Remove from heat and cool.

3. Sprinkle gelatine over water and stir to dissolve, or microwave on MEDIUM for 10 seconds. Cool slightly.

4. Stir gelatine mixture into chocolate mixture, then add sweetener.

5. In a medium bowl, beat egg whites until soft peaks form. Fold into chocolate mixture.

6. Pour into six individual serving dishes. Cover and refrigerate overnight.

7. Serve chilled with strawberries.

YOGHURT FRUIT JELLY

$^2/_3$ cup boiling water
1 packet low-joule orange and mango jelly crystals
$^3/_4$ cup unsweetened pineapple juice
200 g (6$^1/_2$ oz) natural low-fat yoghurt
strawberries to decorate

Makes 4 servings	
Kilojoules per serve	203
Calories per serve	48
Carbohydrate per serve	8 g
Fat	Negligible
Fibre	Negligible

1. Pour boiling water into a bowl and add jelly crystals. Stir until dissolved.

2. Add pineapple juice and stir well.

3. Refrigerate until just beginning to set.

4. Whisk in yoghurt until well blended, then pour into four individual serving dishes.

5. Return to refrigerator until set, then decorate with strawberries and serve.

DRIED FRUIT COMPOTE

200 g (6$^1/_2$ oz) dried fruit salad mix
5 cm (2 in.) strip of lemon rind
2 whole cloves
1$^1/_2$ cups unsweetened apple juice

Makes 4 servings	
Kilojoules per serve	587
Calories per serve	140
Carbohydrate per serve	33 g
Fat	Negligible
Fibre	Very good

1. Place fruit, lemon rind and cloves in a large saucepan on medium heat. Cover with apple juice and slowly bring to the boil.

2. Reduce heat and simmer, covered, for 30 minutes, or until tender.

3. Remove from heat and leave to cool overnight.

4. Remove lemon rind and cloves.

5. Serve warm topped with natural low-fat yoghurt or Cottage Cream (see page 114).

APRICOT AND PASSIONFRUIT FROZEN WHIP

$^2/_3$ cup chopped dried apricots

$^1/_3$ cup water

200 g (6$^1/_2$ oz) vanilla-flavoured diet yoghurt

$^1/_2$ cup skim milk

1 ripe banana, mashed

2 tbsp slivered almonds, toasted

pulp of 2 passionfruit

Makes 6 servings	
Kilojoules per serve	449
Calories per serve	107
Carbohydrate per serve	16 g
Fat	Low
Fibre	Good

1. Place dried apricots and water in a saucepan over medium heat. Cover and simmer until soft, about 3 minutes, or microwave on HIGH for 2–3 minutes. Allow to cool.

2. Process apricots, yoghurt, milk and banana in a blender until smooth.

3. Pour mixture into a 20 cm (8 in.) cake tin, cover with aluminium foil and freeze for several hours, or until set.

4. Transfer to a blender and process until smooth, or churn in an ice-cream maker for 20 minutes.

5. Fold in almonds and passionfruit.

6. Serve immediately.

CAKES, BISCUITS AND SLICES

There's nothing more tantalising than the delicious aroma of cakes baking in the oven. Turning down a slice of fruit cake or apple slice is a pretty difficult task for most of us—and why should we? Fortunately you won't have to say 'no' anymore. Our delicious cake and slice recipes are firm favourites and can be enjoyed by everyone. They all have minimum amounts of added sugar and fat, and most are rich in dietary fibre, so they not only taste good but are quite healthy, too.

Please note if you prefer to use the powdered artificial sweetener Splenda™ and not sugar the recipes will work just as successfully.

APPLE AND APRICOT TEA CAKE

1 tbsp margarine
2 cups self-raising flour
1 egg, beaten
³/₄ cup skim milk
2 tbsp sugar (or artificial sweetener equivalent)
450 g (14¹/₂ oz) canned unsweetened
pie-apple filling
210 g (7 oz) canned unsweetened apricot halves, drained
¹/₂ tsp ground cinnamon

Makes 16 slices	
Kilojoules per serve	172
Calories per serve	41
Carbohydrate per serve	6 g
Fat	Negligible
Fibre	Good

1. In a bowl, rub margarine into flour until crumbly. Combine egg, milk and sugar. Add to dry ingredients and stir until just combined (do not overmix).

2. Pat out half the mixture over base of lightly greased 20 cm (8 in.) springform tin. Spread with apples. Scatter apricots over top. Sprinkle with cinnamon and a little extra sugar to taste.

3. With floured hands, pat out remaining dough into a 20 cm (8 in.) circle on greaseproof paper. Turn onto filling, then press gently to seal. Remove paper. Bake in a moderately hot oven 190°C (375°F) until cooked through and browned, for 50–60 minutes.

4. Cool for about 15 minutes in tin. Remove side of tin and serve warm or cold, as desired. Serve with a small dollop of natural yoghurt if desired.

VERNA'S DATE BRAN CAKE

1 cup Kellogg's All-Bran™
1 cup water
1 egg, beaten
1 tbsp golden syrup
$^1/_3$ cup canola oil
$1^1/_2$ cups plain flour, sifted
2 tbsp brown sugar
1 tsp baking powder
1 tsp baking soda
1 cup chopped dates

Makes 25 slices	
Kilojoules per serve	336
Calories per serve	80
Carbohydrate per serve	14 g
Fat	Low
Fibre	Good

1. In a bowl, place All-Bran™, water, egg, golden syrup and oil. Set aside for 30 minutes.

2. Mix together dry ingredients and dates.

3. Pour in All-Bran™ mixture and blend well, but do not overmix.

4. Pour into a greased 21-cm (8$^1/_4$ in.) loaf pan, then bake in a hot oven 200°C (400°F) for 40–45 minutes, or until top springs back when lightly pressed.

APPLE SAUCE OATMEAL CAKE

2 cups unsweetened apple purée (see Note)

60 g (2 oz) margarine

1 cup rolled oats

2 tbsp sugar (or artificial sweetener equivalent)

2 eggs, beaten

1 tsp vanilla essence

2 cups plain flour

1 tsp baking soda

1 tsp ground cinnamon

Makes 20 slices	
Kilojoules per serve	572
Calories per serve	137
Carbohydrate per serve	20 g
Fat	Low
Fibre	Good

1. Heat apple and margarine over a low heat until margarine has melted.

2. Stir in rolled oats, then set aside for 5 minutes.

3. Add sugar, eggs and vanilla alternately with dry ingredients.

4. Turn batter into a lightly greased 20 cm (8 in.) cake tin.

5. Bake in a moderate oven 180°C (350°F) for 40 minutes or until skewer inserted in centre comes out clean.

Note: Use 425 g (13 1/2 oz) canned unsweetened pie apple mashed with a wooden spoon.

APPLE ROCK CAKES

1 cup self-raising flour
1 cup wholemeal self-raising flour
1 tsp mixed spice
$^1/_4$ cup sugar or 1 tbsp Sucaryl™ (preferable)
$^1/_2$ cup sultanas
2 tbsp mixed peel
$^3/_4$ cup skim or Shape™ milk
1 tbsp canola margarine, melted
1 egg
1 green apple, grated, or 1 cup canned pie apple, diced

Makes 10 rock cakes	
Kilojoules per serve	700
Calories per serve	167
Carbohydrate per serve	30 g
Fat	Low
Fibre	Good

1. In a large bowl, combine flours, mixed spice, sugar, sultanas and mixed peel.

2. In a separate bowl, combine milk, margarine, egg and grated apple. Stir into dry mixture.

3. Spoon heaped tablespoons of mixture onto a greased baking tray.

4. Bake in a moderate oven 180°C (350°F) for 20–25 minutes, or until a skewer inserted in the centre of a cake comes out clean.

OATIES

1¹/₂ cups wholemeal self-raising flour
1¹/₂ cups rolled oats
¹/₂ cup desiccated coconut
¹/₃ cup sultanas
¹/₂ cup currants
³/₄ cup dates
2 tbsp lemon juice
2 tbsp canola oil
1¹/₂ cups skim milk
1 tsp vanilla essence

Makes 25 squares	
Kilojoules per serve	370
Calories per serve	88
Carbohydrate per serve	15 g
Fat	Low
Fibre	Good

1. In a large bowl, combine flour, oats, coconut, sultanas, currants and dates.

2. In a second bowl, whisk together lemon juice, oil, milk and vanilla.

3. Gradually add liquid ingredients to dry ingredients and stir until well combined.

4. Press mixture into a greased non-stick Swiss roll tin.

5. Bake in a moderate oven 180°C (350°F) for 50–60 minutes.

6. Cut into squares while still warm.

COCONUT BUTTONS

1¹/₂ cups self-raising flour
¹/₂ cup custard powder
2 tbsp sugar (or artificial sweetener equivalent)
¹/₂ cup desiccated coconut
60 g (2 oz) margarine
¹/₂ cup skim milk

Makes 35 buttons	
Kilojoules per serve	360
Calories per serve	86
Carbohydrate per serve	12 g
Fat	Low
Fibre	Good

1. Sift flour then mix in custard powder, sugar and coconut.

2. Rub margarine through flour mixture until mixture resembles coarse breadcrumbs.

3. Add milk and mix to a stiff dough.

4. Spoon heaped teaspoonfuls onto lightly greased and floured or non-stick baking trays.

5. Bake in a moderate oven 180°C (350°F) for 12–15 minutes.

6. Remove from trays while still hot.

GOLDEN OAT COOKIES

1 cup rolled oats
1 cup plain flour
2 tbsp sugar (or artificial sweetener equivalent)
³/₄ cup desiccated coconut
60 g (2 oz) margarine
2 tbsp golden syrup
1 tsp baking soda
2 tbsp boiling water

Makes 15 cookies	
Kilojoules per serve	521
Calories per serve	124
Carbohydrate per serve	19 g
Fat	Low
Fibre	Good

1. Mix oats, flour, sugar and coconut together.

2. Melt margarine and golden syrup together.

3. Dissolve baking soda in boiling water then stir into margarine mixture.

4. Pour liquid ingredients into flour mixture. Mix well.

5. Spoon tablespoonfuls onto a lightly greased or non-stick baking tray, then flatten with a fork.

6. Bake in a moderate oven 180°C (350°F) for 15–20 minutes.

CHEWY CHOC CHIP COOKIES

50 g (1½ oz) margarine
⅓ cup brown sugar
1 egg, beaten
1 cup self-raising flour
½ cup choc chips
⅓ cup slivered almonds

Makes 18 cookies	
Kilojoules per serve	391
Calories per serve	93
Carbohydrate per serve	12 g
Fat	Moderate
Fibre	Low

1.   Cream margarine and sugar until pale in colour. Add egg and beat well.

2.   Add flour, then choc chips and almonds. Mix well.

3.   Bake in a moderate oven 180°C (350°F) for 10 minutes. Stand for a few minutes before removing from trays.

REDSKIN BISCUITS

60 g (2 oz) margarine
2 tbsp sugar (or artificial sweetener equivalent)
1 egg
1 tsp vanilla essence
1 cup plain flour, sifted
½ cup raw peanuts, roughly chopped

Makes 15 biscuits	
Kilojoules per serve	372
Calories per serve	89
Carbohydrate per serve	2 g
Fat	Low
Fibre	Good

1.   Cream margarine and sugar, then add egg and vanilla. Beat well.

2.   Mix in sifted flour and peanuts.

3.   Spoon heaped teaspoonfuls of mixture onto lightly greased or non-stick oven trays. Flatten lightly with a fork.

4.   Bake in a moderate oven 180°C (350°F) for 10–15 minutes.

5.   Allow to cool slightly before removing from tray.

MUESLI BARS

1¹/₂ cups wholemeal self-raising flour

¹/₂ cup rolled oats

60 g (2 oz) chopped roasted almonds

1 tbsp sesame seeds, toasted

¹/₂ cup sultanas

¹/₂ cup currants

¹/₂ cup raw sugar

¹/₂ cup skim-milk powder

1 cup natural low-fat yoghurt

¹/₄ cup honey

4 tbsp margarine

Makes approximately 24 bars	
Kilojoules per serve	580
Calories per serve	138
Carbohydrate per serve	20 g
Fat	Low
Fibre	Very good

1. Mix dry ingredients together, then make a well and pour in the yoghurt.

2. Melt honey and margarine together, then pour on to the yoghurt.

3. Mix with a wooden spoon until well combined.

4. Spread mixture into a lightly greased lamington tray, using wet hands to press down firmly.

5. Bake in a hot oven 200°C (400°F) for 15–20 minutes.

6. Cut into bars when cool.

PINA COLADA SQUARES

Base

1 cup plain flour
1 tsp baking powder
$^1/_4$ tsp salt
$^1/_4$ cup margarine
1 egg, separated
$^1/_4$ cup Shape™ milk

Makes 16 squares	
Kilojoules per serve	453
Calories per serve	108
Carbohydrate per serve	13 g
Fat	Low
Fibre	Good

1. Combine flour, baking powder and salt in a bowl.
2. Cut in margarine until mixture is crumbly.
3. Beat egg yolk and milk together with a fork.
4. Stir into flour mixture.
5. Press an even layer onto the bottom of a lamington cake tin.

Filling

400 ml (13 fl oz) canned unsweetened crushed pineapple and juice
2 tbsp cornflour
2 tsp almond essence
1 tsp vanilla essence
1 tsp Sucaryl™

1. Combine crushed pineapple and juice and cornflour in a saucepan, mixing well.
2. Stir over medium heat until mixture boils and thickens.
3. Stir in almond essence, vanilla and Sucaryl™.
4. Pour over base.

Topping

$^1/_4$ tsp cream of tartar
1 tbsp sugar
1 cup shredded coconut

1. Beat remaining egg white and cream of tartar until frothy.
2. Add sugar and beat until soft peaks form.
3. Fold in coconut.
4. Spread evenly and carefully over filling.
5. Press down lightly with a fork.
6. Bake in a moderate oven 180°C (350°F) for 30 minutes until top is golden brown.
    Cool and cut into squares.

MUFFINS, SCONES AND LOAVES

For those of us without a sweet tooth, yet looking for something to eat with a cup of tea or coffee, a slice of banana bread or perhaps a fruit muffin might be just what you are looking for.

Make sure you spread with reduced-fat margarine or cream cheese to keep the fat and kilojoule content down.

PEACH AND CINNAMON MUFFINS

1$^1/_2$ cups plain, wholemeal flour
$^2/_3$ cup rolled oats
$^1/_2$ tsp nutmeg
$^1/_4$ tsp cinnamon
1$^1/_2$ tbsp brown sugar
$^1/_2$ cup unsweetened pie peaches
1 cup buttermilk
1 small egg, beaten
2 tsp canola oil

Makes 12 muffins	
Kilojoules per serve	435
Calories per serve	104
Carbohydrate per serve	16 g
Fat	Low
Fibre	Good

1. Place flour, oats, nutmeg, cinnamon and brown sugar in a mixing bowl.

2. Stir in peaches.

3. Mix buttermilk, egg and oil together in a separate bowl, then stir into peach mixture with a few swift strokes.

4. Spoon into lightly greased muffin tins and bake in a moderate oven 180°C (350°F) for 30–40 minutes.

5. Serve warm.

LEMON AND POPPY SEED MUFFINS

1¹/₂ tbsp canola oil

¹/₄ cup sugar or 1 tbsp Sucaryl™ (preferable)

1 egg, lightly beaten

³/₄ cup skim or Shape™ milk

rind and juice of 1 lemon

¹/₄ cup poppy seeds

1 cup self-raising flour

1 cup wholemeal self-raising flour

¹/₂ cup sultanas

Makes 16 muffins	
Kilojoules per serve	460
Calories per serve	109
Carbohydrate per serve	15 g
Fat	Low
Fibre	Low

1. Mix oil, sugar, egg, milk, lemon juice and rind and poppy seeds in a large bowl.

2. Combine flours and sultanas in a separate bowl, then gently fold into wet ingredients, stirring 16 times. Place in non-stick or lightly greased muffin tins.

3. Bake in a hot oven 200°C (400°F) for 25 minutes, or until top springs back when lightly pressed.

BANANA MUFFINS

¹/₄ cup canola oil

2 medium bananas, mashed

1 egg, lightly beaten

1 tsp vanilla essence

1 cup Kellogg's All-Bran™ cereal

1 cup plain flour

1 cup wholemeal self-raising flour

¹/₂ tsp baking powder

¹/₄ cup raisins, chopped

Makes 15 muffins	
Kilojoules per serve	526
Calories per serve	125
Carbohydrate per serve	19 g
Fat	Low
Fibre	Good

1. Combine oil, bananas, egg, vanilla essence and All-Bran™ in a large bowl. Allow to stand for 5 minutes.

2. Sift together plain flour, wholemeal flour and baking powder.

3. Add dry ingredients to All-Bran™ mixture and stir until just combined.

4. Fold in raisins.

5. Spoon batter into lightly greased muffin tins, filling to about ³/₄ full.

6. Bake in a moderate oven 180°C (350°F) for 20–25 minutes, or until golden brown.

JENI'S COTTAGE CHEESE TEA BREAD

250 g (8 oz) cottage cheese

150 g (4¹/₂ oz) brown sugar

3 eggs, beaten

50 g (1¹/₂ oz) walnuts

100 g (3¹/₂ oz) pitted dates, coarsely chopped

³/₄ cup self-raising flour

1 cup wholemeal self-raising flour

Kilojoules per serve	619
Calories per serve	147
Carbohydrate per serve	23 g
Fat	Low
Fibre	Good

1. Push cottage cheese through a sieve into a bowl, add brown sugar and beat until creamy.

2. Add eggs and beat well.

3. Coarsely chop walnuts, leaving 5–6 whole for decoration.

4. Add chopped walnuts and dates to mixture.

5. Fold in flours.

6. Pour into a lightly greased 1 kg (2 lb) loaf tin. Press reserved whole walnuts on top.

7. Bake in moderate oven 180°C (350°F) for 45–50 minutes.

YOGHURT PIKELETS

1 egg

1 cup skim milk

1 tsp baking powder

2 tsp canola oil

1¹/₂ cups wholemeal self-raising flour

400 g (13 oz) low-fat berry-flavoured yoghurt

Makes 30 pikelets (2 per serve)	
Kilojoules per serve	388
Calories per serve	93
Carbohydrate per serve	15 g
Fat	Low
Fibre	Good

1. Blend egg with milk, baking powder, oil, flour and half the yoghurt, until smooth.

2. Drop tablespoonfuls of batter onto a heated, lightly greased or non-stick frying pan.

3. Cook until surface bubbles appear then turn and brown on other side.

4. Serve hot with reserved fruit yoghurt.

PINEAPPLE CORN BREAD

$^2/_3$ cup self-raising flour
1 cup yellow cornmeal
1 egg, beaten
3 tbsp sugar (or artificial sweetener equivalent)
$^1/_2$ cup unsweetened crushed pineapple
$^1/_2$ cup skim milk
$^1/_2$ cup unsweetened pineapple juice
60 g (2 oz) margarine, melted

Makes 15 slices	
Kilojoules per serve	518
Calories per serve	124
Carbohydrate per serve	18 g
Fat	Low
Fibre	Good

1. Sift flour then stir in remaining ingredients.

2. Pour into a lightly greased 20 x 10 cm (8 x 4 in.) loaf tin.

3. Bake in a hot oven 200°C (400°F) for 30–40 minutes or until a skewer inserted into the centre comes out clean.

4. Serve warm.

ITALIAN TOMATO SCONES

2 tbsp margarine
2 cups self-raising flour
2 tbsp grated parmesan cheese
$^2/_3$ cup unsweetened tomato juice
skim milk for glazing

Makes 12 scones	
Kilojoules per serve	626
Calories per serve	150
Carbohydrate per serve	18 g
Fat	Low
Fibre	Good

1. Rub margarine through flour with fingertips. Add cheese.

2. Make a well in centre of flour mixture, pour in tomato juice then mix quickly and lightly to form a soft dough.

3. Roll out on a floured board to 2 cm ($^3/_4$ in.) thickness, then cut into rounds with a 5 cm (2 in.) cutter.

4. Place scones on lightly greased oven tray, and brush tops with skim milk.

5. Bake in a hot oven 230°C (450°F) for 15 minutes.

WHOLEMEAL DATE SCONES

2 cups self-raising flour
$^1/_2$ cup unprocessed bran
$^1/_2$ tsp ground ginger
50 g (1$^1/_2$ oz) margarine
$^1/_4$ cup chopped dates
1 cup skim milk

Makes 14 scones	
Kilojoules per serve	549
Calories per serve	131
Carbohydrate per serve	20 g
Fat	Low
Fibre	Very good

1. Sift flour then add unprocessed bran and ginger.

2. Rub margarine into dry ingredients with fingertips.

3. Stir in dates then add enough milk to make a soft dough.

4. Knead lightly on a floured board. Roll out dough to 2 cm ($^3/_4$ in.) thickness, then cut into 14 pieces.

5. Place on a lightly greased or non-stick baking tray.

6. Bake in a very hot oven 250°C (500°F) for 10–15 minutes.

KELLOGG'S BANANA BRAN BREAD

Recipe courtesy of Kellogg Australia

4 medium bananas, mashed
³/₄ cup skim milk
1 cup Kellogg's All-Bran™
60 g (2 oz) margarine, softened
2 eggs
1 cup self-raising flour
1 cup wholemeal self-raising flour
1 tbsp walnuts, chopped

Makes 17 slices	
Kilojoules per serve	616
Calories per serve	147
Carbohydrate per serve	20 g
Fat	Low
Fibre	Very good

1. Combine mashed bananas, skim milk and All-Bran™, then let stand for about 10 minutes or until cereal has softened.

2. In a separate bowl beat margarine and eggs together then stir in cereal mixture.

3. Sift flours then add to other ingredients with walnuts and mix well.

4. Pour batter into a lightly greased or non-stick 21 cm (8¹/₄ in.) loaf tin.

5. Bake in a moderate oven 180°C (350°F) for 50 minutes or until skewer inserted in centre comes out clean.

6. Allow to cool for 10 minutes before removing from tin.

DIPS, SPREADS AND SAUCES

A simple meal can often be turned into a gourmet's delight with the addition of an interesting sauce, dressing or topping. You can disguise a culinary flop or entice a child (grown-up ones too!) to eat vegetables or other disliked foods if they are topped or coated with a tasty sauce.

If you're watching your weight but love dips and spreads, our recipes will surely please your palate and your waistline since they are all low in fat and kilojoules.

TANGY VEGETABLE SAUCE

4 large carrots

2 large onions

2 large capsicums

$^1/_2$ bunch celery

800 g (1 lb 9$^1/_2$ oz) canned peeled tomatoes

1 cup tomato sauce

2 tbsp tomato paste

salt and freshly ground pepper to taste

Makes 5 cups	
Kilojoules per serve	341
Calories per serve	82
Carbohydrate per serve	16 g
Fat	Negligible
Fibre	Very good

1. Chop carrots, onions, capsicums and celery coarsely, then place into a large saucepan.

2. Add tomatoes, tomato sauce, tomato paste and seasonings.

3. Simmer for about 30 minutes or until vegetables are tender and sauce is slightly thickened.

4. Serve hot or cold with any cooked pasta, legumes, rice, etc.

CREAMY TOFU DRESSING

1 packet (300 g/9$^1/_2$ oz) soft tofu
2 tbsp white vinegar
1 tsp Dijon mustard
1 tsp soy sauce
$^1/_2$ tsp dried parsley
$^1/_4$ tsp minced garlic

Makes 1$^1/_2$ cups	
Kilojoules per serve	212
Calories per serve	54
Carbohydrate per serve	Nil
Fat	Negligible
Fibre	Nil

1. Drain tofu then mash with a fork until smooth.

2. Blend in remaining ingredients.

3. Chill well before serving.

4. Store in refrigerator in a screw-top jar. Use in place of mayonnaise.

GREEN PEA PATÉ

1 cup frozen green peas, thawed
250 g (8 oz) cottage cheese
$^1/_2$ small onion, chopped
1 tbsp lemon juice
salt and ground black pepper to taste

Makes 1$^1/_2$ cups	
Kilojoules per serve	200
Calories per serve	48
Carbohydrate per serve	2 g
Fat	Negligible
Fibre	Good

1. In a blender or food processor, blend all ingredients until thick and smooth.

2. Season to taste then chill at least 1 hour before serving.

3. Serve with crisp crackers, toast or vegetable crudités.

SARDINE SPREAD

125 g (4 oz) sardines in tomato sauce, mashed
250 g (8 oz) low-fat cream cheese
1 tbsp low-joule Italian dressing
ground pepper to taste
1 tbsp chopped parsley

Makes 2 cups	
Kilojoules per serve	406
Calories per serve	97
Carbohydrate per serve	Nil
Fat	Low
Fibre	Nil

1. Blend all ingredients. Chill.

2. Serve as sandwich spread or with crackers, etc.

HERBED YOGHURT DRESSING

200 g (6$^1/_2$ oz) natural low-fat yoghurt
$^1/_2$ cup buttermilk
1 tbsp parsley, chopped
$^1/_2$ tsp each thyme, tarragon and dill
1 small clove garlic, crushed
1 tsp vinegar
$^1/_2$ tsp Worcestershire sauce

Makes 1$^1/_2$ cups	
Kilojoules per serve	157
Calories per serve	37
Carbohydrate per serve	4 g
Fat	Negligible
Fibre	Nil

1. Blend all ingredients or alternatively shake in a screw-top jar.

2. Allow to chill for at least 2 hours to develop flavour before serving.

3. Serve chilled with salads or vegetables.

TARTARE CRAB SPREAD

170 g (5^1/$_2$ oz) canned crab meat
^{1}/$_2$ cup finely chopped celery
2 tbsp finely chopped gherkin
2 tsp capers, chopped
^{1}/$_4$ cup low-fat mayonnaise
2 tbsp natural low-fat yoghurt
2 tsp lemon juice
salt and ground black pepper to taste

Makes 1^1/$_2$ cups	
Kilojoules per serve	224
Calories per serve	54
Carbohydrate per serve	3 g
Fat	Negligible
Fibre	Nil

1. Drain and flake crab meat.

2. Combine with remaining ingredients, then chill.

3. Serve as a dip or spread.

COTTAGE CREAM

250 g (8 oz) cottage cheese
100 g (3^1/$_2$ oz) natural low-fat yoghurt
1 tbsp lemon juice
1 tbsp lemon rind, finely grated
2 tsp sugar (or 1 sachet of Equal™)

Makes 1^1/$_2$ cups	
Kilojoules per serve	223
Calories per serve	53
Carbohydrate per serve	4 g
Fat	Negligible
Fibre	Nil

1. Blend cottage cheese, yoghurt, lemon juice and rind until smooth.

2. Sweeten to taste. Chill.

3. Serve as topping for fruit salad, etc., or eliminate sweetener and use as a topping or dressing for vegetables or salads.

TANGY ORANGE SAUCE

1 tbsp custard powder
1 tbsp margarine
1 cup orange juice
1 tbsp sugar (or 1 sachet of Equal™)

Makes 1½ cups (½ cup per serve)	
Kilojoules per serve	451
Calories per serve	108
Carbohydrate per serve	14 g
Fat	Low
Fibre	Nil

1. In a small saucepan combine custard powder, margarine and orange juice.

2. Cook over a low heat, stirring constantly until thickened and smooth.

3. Remove from heat and sweeten to taste.

4. Serve warm over vanilla ice-cream or sliced bananas and yoghurt, etc.

CHOCOLATE SAUCE

1 tbsp cocoa
1 tbsp custard powder
1 tsp vanilla essence
1 cup evaporated skim milk
1 tbsp margarine
1 tbsp sugar (or artificial sweetener equivalent)

Makes 1 cup (2 tbsp per serve)	
Kilojoules per serve	307
Calories per serve	73
Carbohydrate per serve	9 g
Fat	Negligible
Fibre	Nil

1. In a small saucepan combine cocoa, custard powder, vanilla, milk, margarine and sugar.

2. Cook gently over a low heat, stirring constantly until thickened and smooth.

3. Remove from heat.

4. Serve warm over vanilla ice-cream, sliced pears, etc.

SMOKED OYSTER DIP

250 g (8 oz) low-fat cream cheese
1½ tsp lemon juice
pinch cayenne pepper
3 tbsp finely chopped shallots (green onions)
100 g (3½ oz) canned smoked oysters,
finely chopped
3 tsp dry vermouth or white wine
¼ cup skim milk

Makes 1½ cups	
Kilojoules per serve	316
Calories per serve	75
Carbohydrate per serve	Negligible
Fat	Low
Fibre	Nil

1. Combine cheese, juice and seasoning.

2. Add shallots and oysters, and mix well.

3. Add vermouth and enough milk to make a soft dipping consistency.

4. Chill before serving with crisp celery sticks or crackers.

APRICOT CONSERVE

300 g (9½ oz) dried apricots, chopped
1 cup orange juice
2 cooking apples, peeled, cored and sliced
Equal™ (sweetener) to taste

Makes 2 to 3 small jars	
Kilojoules per serve	253
Calories per serve	61
Carbohydrate per serve	14 g
Fat	Nil
Fibre	Very good

1. Place apricots, juice and apples in a saucepan, then bring to the boil.

2. Reduce heat then cook gently, uncovered, stirring frequently until fruit is very soft and mixture has thickened.

3. Sweeten if desired.

4. Pour into glass jars. Cover to seal.

5. Store in refrigerator.

PRUNE AND APPLE SPREAD

600 g (1 lb 3½ oz) prunes, pitted and chopped
2 cups apple juice
4 cooking apples, peeled, cored and sliced

Makes 4 to 6 small jars	
Kilojoules per serve	346
Calories per serve	83
Carbohydrate per serve	20 g
Fat	Nil
Fibre	Very good

1. Place all ingredients in a large saucepan.

2. Cook for 20–30 minutes over low heat until mixture has formed a thick, spreadable consistency.

3. Pour into glass jars. Cover to seal.

4. Store in refrigerator.

LESLEY'S SALMON DIP

210 g (6¾ oz) canned pink salmon
200 g (6½ oz) natural low-fat yoghurt
1 small cucumber, peeled and finely diced
2 tsp lemon juice
1 tbsp chopped chives
salt and ground pepper to taste

Makes 1 cup	
Kilojoules per serve	347
Calories per serve	83
Carbohydrate per serve	Negligible
Fat	Low
Fibre	Good

1. Drain salmon, remove bones and then mash with a fork.

2. Mix in remaining ingredients. Chill.

3. Serve with vegetable crudités, crisp toast fingers or crackers.

PASKA (SIMA'S RUSSIAN CHEESE)

500 g (1 lb) low-fat farm cheese (see Note)

$^1/_2$ cup mixed dried fruit

1 egg, lightly beaten

1 tbsp lemon rind, grated

$^1/_2$ tsp vanilla essence

2 sachets Equal™

Makes 8 to 10 servings	
Kilojoules per serve	400
Calories per serve	96
Carbohydrate per serve	Negligible
Fat	Low
Fibre	Negligible

1. With your hands mix together cheese, fruit, egg, rind, vanilla and sweetener.

2. Press into a deep mould (e.g. a small clean flower pot) lined with two layers of plastic wrap.

3. Chill for several hours to develop flavour before serving.

4. Invert onto a serving platter and serve in small slices as an after-dinner 'sweet'.

Note: Low-fat farm cheese is available from most delicatessens.

ENTERTAINING

Preparing a menu for a guest who has diabetes can be a cause for concern if you're not accustomed to doing so. In fact, it's not difficult if you keep in mind these basic dietary principles:

- *ensure adequate complex carbohydrates are served, e.g. pasta, rice, potato, bread rolls, etc.*
- *ensure your meal contains a minimal amount of fat, i.e. avoid fried foods, rich creamy sauces, cheesy toppings, pastry, etc.*
- *avoid nuts, crisps, salami and olive starters. Serve low-fat cheese, dips, crudités, bread and crackers.*
- *no foods are forbidden, therefore it's not necessary to include special 'diabetic foods'.*
- *simple desserts such as fresh fruit salad and ice-cream are preferable to cheese and biscuits, which are high in fat, to end your meal.*

SAMPLE NO-FUSS DINNER PARTY MENU

SUMMER

Entrée
Spinach parsley fettuccine

Main course
Baked spicy chicken
Savoury rice bake
Green and gold salad

Dessert
Apricot and passionfruit frozen whip

WINTER

Entrée
Easy fish soup

Main course
Jill's crusty lamb
Microwave potato and carrot bake
Lemony vegetables with dill

Dessert
Dried fruit compote
Cottage cream

AT CHRISTMAS TIME

Being on a special diet at Christmas is not a happy prospect for anyone. Thankfully the dietary recommendations for diabetes are a lot more flexible these days, so everyone can enjoy and celebrate this special time of year.

Certainly it is important to take medication as usual, and, of course, eat as close to usual meal times as possible, but there's no need to miss out on all the traditional goodies enjoyed by your family and friends to celebrate Christmas.

You can enjoy roasts, seafoods, special pastas or pies, all kinds of vegetables and salads, fresh fruits, ice-cream and special puddings. Eating a small amount of all that is served will not be harmful. So relax and enjoy. Eat, drink and celebrate—we all deserve a treat at this special time of year.

BUNTY'S DIVINE FRUIT CAKE

425 g (13½ oz) canned unsweetened
pineapple pieces, drained
1 orange, rind grated and juice reserved
1 lemon, rind grated and juice reserved
1 cup sultanas
1 cup currants
1 cup pitted dates, chopped
1½ cups strong, hot brewed tea
2 eggs
125 g (4 oz) margarine, melted
1 cup walnuts, chopped
2½ cups wholemeal self-raising flour
¼ cup dry sherry (optional)

Makes 44 servings	
Kilojoules per serve	440
Calories per serve	105
Carbohydrate per serve	15 g
Fat	Low
Fibre	Good

1. In a large bowl combine pineapple with reserved juice from orange and lemon, dried
    fruits and grated rind. Add hot tea. Let mixture stand overnight to soak.

2. Next day, beat eggs into fruit mixture. Stir in margarine and nuts. Sift in the flour,
    adding husks from sifter to bowl. Mix well until combined.

3. Turn mixture into a deep, lightly greased and paper-lined 23 cm (9 in.) round cake
    tin. Smooth over surface with wet fingers.

4. Bake in oven 160°C (315°F) for approximately 2½–3 hours or until a skewer inserted
    into centre comes out clean.

5. Cool before turning out onto wire rack. If desired, drizzle or brush sherry over cake
    while still warm, then cover with a clean tea towel. Cool completely.

CHRISTMAS PUDDING

120 g (4 oz) currants
100 g (3¹/₂ oz) sultanas
100 g (3¹/₂ oz) raisins
¹/₂ cup orange juice
1 tsp mixed spice
¹/₂ tsp nutmeg
¹/₂ tsp cinnamon
¹/₂ tsp ground ginger
grated rind of 1 lemon
¹/₄ cup brandy
¹/₂ cup plain wholemeal flour
¹/₄ tsp baking soda
1¹/₂ cups wholemeal breadcrumbs
2 medium bananas, mashed
1 large carrot
1 egg, beaten
1 medium green apple, grated
3 tbsp evaporated skim milk
2 tbsp margarine, melted

Makes 12 servings	
Kilojoules per serve	768
Calories per serve	184
Carbohydrate per serve	30 g
Fat	Low
Fibre	Very good

1. Place dried fruit, juice, spices and rind in a large saucepan, then simmer gently until fruit is soft and plump. Cool, add brandy then leave to stand overnight.

2. Sift together flour and soda. Return bran husks from sifter to bowl, then stir into fruit mixture with breadcrumbs, bananas, carrot, egg, apple, milk and melted margarine.

3. Pour mixture into lightly greased pudding basin, then steam for 3 hours.

4. Serve with custard flavoured with a little brandy or whisky.

INDEX OF RECIPE NAMES

GENERAL INDEX